jealousy SURVIVAL GUIDE

How to feel safe, happy, and secure in an open relationship

Kitty Chambliss, CPC, ELI-MP

Get free resources and join our community at:
LovingWithoutBoundaries.com

Legal Information

© 2017 Loving Without Boundaries. All Rights Reserved. "Jealousy Survival Guide: How to feel safe, happy, and secure in an open relationship: First Edition". This book may not be reproduced in any form, in whole or in part, without written permission from the author. It's easy to get permission; just drop an email to kitty@lovingwithoutboundaries.com.

Quotes from pp. 147, 158, 163–4 from EMOTIONAL BLACKMAIL by SUSAN FORWARD and DONNA FRAZIER. © 1997 by Susan Forward. Reprinted by permission of HarperCollins Publishers.

Concepts for the Constructive Jealousy DC3 Framework are being shared, adapted, and provided in this publication with permission from Kelly Cookson and his wife, Andrea via the Creative Commons license that can be found at: creativecommons.org/licenses/by-nc/4.0/. For further reading, additional informational downloads, and instruction, please go to kellycookson.info.

Various quotations are shared in this publication for motivational and inspirational purposes. For more information about Karen Salmansohn, please visit notsalmon.com. For more information about Bruce Schneider, founder of the *Institute for Professional Excellence in Coaching (IPEC)*, please visit, ipeccoaching.com.

Editor: Dr. Elisabeth Sheff (elisabethsheff.com)
Book Cover and Interior Design: Giant Leaps Creative LLC (giantleapscreative.com)

This publication is written to speak to your emotional intelligence and your common sense, and should not be used as a substitute. Nor is it a substitute for the advice of your doctor, therapist, guardian angel, dog, cat, or any other of your trusted advisors, personal, professional, or spiritual.

If you would like to invite the author to speak at an event for your organization, please make contact via the Loving Without Boundaries website at lovingwithoutboundaries.com.

Printed by CreateSpace, An Amazon.com Company. Available from Amazon.com, on Kindle, and other online stores.

This book is dedicated to:

... the Loving Without Boundaries (LWB) community. Your courage, compassion, and empathetic spirit inspires me daily. I lovingly create this book for you and your spectacularly brave journey.

... my beautiful-from-the-inside-out partners — my loving, fantastic husband + my sweet beloved nesting partner. You are both two of my biggest supporters, cheerleaders, and uber fans. My heart is bursting for you and I am filled with gratitude for your generous, compassionate, and kind love.

ACKNOWLEDGEMENTS

This book would not be possible without the love, support, guidance, and cheerleading of so many wonderful people. I whole-heartedly want to especially thank the following:

Many of the concepts of "Constructive Jealousy" related and shared here are generously donated by Kelly Cookson. I hold Kelly in high regard for his permission to share this powerful teaching, which reflects some of his life work and achievements surrounding the emotion of jealousy and how it interplays with those practicing consensual non-monogamy and polyamory.

Susan Forward and Donna Frazier's book *Emotional Blackmail* was a pivotal contribution to my own journey in navigating challenging relationships and emotions. I'm amazed by how relevant the concepts in this 1990s book are today to the reactions we all have to highly charged emotions such as jealousy. Special thanks to Peter London at HarperCollins Publishing for his guidance through the permissions request process.

After college, I met an incredible woman, Karen Salmansohn when she was doing a reading in Philadelphia for her book: *How To Succeed in Business Without A Penis*. Later in life, I decided to hire her as my professional mentor for an all-day working session to help me take my Loving Without Boundaries (LWB) mission to the next level. Her belief in me and her skillful guidance helped me to pull up my bootstraps and keep sailing higher with my work. Thank you for believing in me and my work, Karen, and for inspiring me to "Give it all I've got!" with my unique gifts.

To my editor, friend, colleague, and mentor, Dr. Elisabeth Sheff, "You rock, you baller!" This book would not be possible without her outstanding editing skills as well as deep understanding and research of the polyamorous community. Thank you from the bottom of my heart for being my editor and proofreader, for writing the insightful and powerful foreword to this work, and for just being plain awesome.

I am extremely grateful to the *Institute for Professional Excellence in Coaching (IPEC)* coaching community and teachers, as well as its founder Bruce Schneider, who is quoted throughout this book. The teaching, the concepts, and especially the community have been an unwavering source of support for me on my journey.

One of my mentors, the late Scott Dinsmore — creator of Live Your Legend (LYL) — is forever in my heart and my soul. Scott, his wife Chelsea, and so many others in the LYL community have supported my efforts from day one of not only my LWB journey, but my oftentimes scary entrepreneurial journey. I especially want to thank some of my business coaches, Nazrin Murphie, Leah Hynes, and Steven Briginshaw for their support, guidance, encouragement, and much needed advice, as well as the larger LYL community of inspiring souls.

The amazing presenters and information at the World Domination Summit, created by Chris Guillebeau, significantly influenced this book. I have met so many wonderful people at this event that have either cheered me on, inspired me, lit a fire under my fanny, or generally made me believe in myself, my abilities, and my mission.

To my highly supportive friends and LWB community members, Ed, Blair, Becky, Chris, and Kerri, THANK YOU for the hours you have put in and the words and advice you have shared to help make LWB, the workshops, and tools what they are today.

To my extended family members and friends Sarah, Melissa, Pauline, Jeanne, and Jensina, thank you for your acceptance, your unconditional love, your understanding, your advice, your encouragement, and especially for your belief in me.

Lastly to my beloved partners, Eric and Rob, I LOVE YOU BOTH! I cherish singing it from the mountaintops and in this book. Your belief in me, your pride in my work, your endless support, your words of advice, your patience, your hugs, your kisses, your holding my hand, your traveling around the world to hear me speak my message to as many people as I can have all been crucially important to me and my journey... I don't have enough words to thank you. I am welling up with tears as I write this. I hope you know how much I love you.

FOREWORD

Jealousy can have an enormous impact on some people, so it is no surprise that people (especially those who practice consensual non-monogamy) think, talk, and write about it quite a bit. In *Jealousy Survival Guide*, Kitty Chambliss does the homework for you and collects the best tidbits on life and emotions to give you inspiration and provide tools to gain and practice new skills. Combining her own life experience with these pearls of wisdom, Kitty focuses on jealousy in consensually non-monogamous relationships, what it is, how it expresses, and specific ways to manage it. Kitty's lack of judgmentalism, frank discussion of her own struggles with jealousy, and focus on specific skills and techniques — without a shred of blame — makes *Jealousy Survival Guide* a delightfully useful read for anyone struggling with jealousy or consensually non-monogamous relationships and polyamory.

As a researcher of polyamory, coach for folks struggling with challenges in polyamorous or kinky relationships, and survivor of polyamory gone incredibly wrong, I have witnessed the many ways in which jealousy can damage consensually non-monogamous relationships. In research, I have heard from people in polyamorous relationships across the United States that they struggle with jealousy with partners, lovers, friends, and family. Assistance navigating the challenges of jealousy is one of the primary reasons that my clients seek out relationship coaching.

Jealousy also destroyed my first polyamorous relationship — but if you use these tools and skills you do not have to experience the same wrenching conclusion I did. When I was 22, I fell in love with a man who told me he never wanted to be monogamous or get married, and we spent the next 10 years talking about it incessantly. He wanted me to find us a woman who would join us to form a triad (classic Unicorn Hunting, though we did not know what it was called at the time), and I was incredibly reluctant. In these discussions, we assumed that my fear of polyamory would translate as jealousy if he connected with someone else. We both thought that he would be fine with me connecting with someone else because he was, as he told me over and over, "poly to the bone."

Turns out, bone meant the erection he got thinking about us with another woman. When I did fall in love with someone else and that person was a man, my then-partner lost it completely. His jealousy was out of control, and so incredibly overwhelming for him that he was willing to marry me and be monogamous even though that was abhorrent to him before someone else wanted me. By that time however, I was angry (OK, furious) that he had pushed for 10 years for polyamory when I did not want it, but swiftly pivoted to monogamy as soon as he had to face his own jealousy. By externalizing his jealousy and trying to make it into my problem instead of learning to tolerate it himself, he poisoned our relationship and drove me away.

If he had been able to read this excellent book and learn the practical advice and exercises it contains, I have a feeling that everything would have been different for us. We might still be together today! The advice in this book is excellent for people struggling with jealousy, and if you use these tools and practice the exercises contained in this valuable volume, you could have a much better outcome than we did with jealousy running rampant. Not only could you learn to tolerate your feelings, but you could enjoy personal growth and happier relationships.

Thank you, Kitty Chambliss, for writing this incredibly helpful book that is fast to read and easy to use! It can provide countless relationships — polyamorous or not — with the tools they need to get over difficult times and thrive with new skills.

Dr. Elisabeth "Eli" Sheff
Author of *The Polyamorists Next Door*, *Stories from the Polycule*, and *When Someone You Love is Polyamorous*

Table Of Contents

ACKNOWLEDGEMENTS 4

FOREWORD 7

— SECTION I: GETTING READY —

INTRODUCTION
Why You Should Read This Book 12

CHAPTER 1
Pre-Game Prep: Positive Mindset 24

CHAPTER 2
Jealousy Game Plan: S.O.S. 35

— SECTION II: STRATEGIES FOR DEALING WITH JEALOUSY —

CHAPTER 3
Strategy One: Defusion 47

CHAPTER 4
Strategy Two: Compassion 54

CHAPTER 5
Strategy Three: Commitment To Your Core Personal Values 62

CHAPTER 6
Strategy Four: Communication 68

— SECTION III: NOW WHAT? —

CHAPTER 7
Putting It All Together 93

RESOURCES 100

BIBLIOGRAPHY 102

ABOUT THE AUTHOR 103

SECTION I

Why You Should Read This Book

So you want to embark on creating the possibility of having an open, ethically non-monogamous relationship, but you are concerned about the elephant in the consensual non-monogamy living room — jealousy. How will you cope?

Jealousy happens. Simply experiencing jealousy is not the problem. The real problem is that our society teaches us to express jealousy in destructive ways. If you would like to learn how to express jealousy in a constructive way, then this book could be very useful for you.

Let's face it: feeling challenging emotions like jealousy and dealing with them in destructive ways can potentially damage our relationships and connections with those that we love, even if we are living a monogamous life or a polyamorous / consensually non-monogamous life.

The Bad News

Jealousy can hijack your brain, make you feel incredibly uncomfortable, and leave you questioning yourself and your relationships. It is an emotion that we will all feel from time to time. We can't escape it. Sure, some feel jealousy or other emotions more intensely than others. Emotions are messengers to us, and a fundamental part of our basic humanity, so it is extremely helpful to learn to swim through and navigate them, whether they are enjoyable emotions or not.

The Good News

You can learn to not only manage the emotion of jealousy, but even to use it to your advantage to build emotional intimacy with your partners, learn, grow, and rock your relationships in the process! I can show you how if you follow the steps outlined here in this book.

Why Listen to Me?

I have been where you might be right now with all of those wonky feelings — jealousy and fear galore — trying to truly enjoy my polyamorous relationships yet struggling with challenging and stressful emotions. Heck, I still deal with them from time to time! Hey, I'm human just like you!

But we can all learn techniques and strategies for not only surviving these stressful emotions, but thriving with them! I can teach you how with time-proven methods that I have used myself — so I know they work! Learning to manage challenging emotions is a practice, much like how we practice meditation or any new skill, and you can do it too.

My name is Kitty Chambliss, and I've been in consensually non-monogamous relationships for over 12 years, and I have identified as polyamorous for more than five years. I have done the research. I have read the books. I have cried in the corner or hidden under the covers and wondered how in the heck I was going to get past these difficult emotions and experiences. Yet I have survived and come to love life even more! Let me show you how you can have all of the love, compassion, connection, and intimacy in your life that you desire. Why just walk numbly through mediocre relationships — or worse, fight and argue with your loves — when you can ROCK your relationships?! Don't settle. Get real with yourself and your life's goals. Make your relationships AWESOME! Why? Because you can!

OVERVIEW OF THE BOOK

This chapter defines jealousy and identifies some of its triggers and the ways in which people tend to react to jealousy. Then there are three sections. Section I prepares readers to face their jealousy. Chapter one guides readers through creating a positive mindset to learn new skills, and chapter two offers baseline tools such as S.O.S. and ways to observe jealousy. Section II details four strategies for dealing with jealousy. The first strategy, defusion, is the topic of chapter three, and chapter four focuses on the second strategy, compassion. In chapter five we explore the third strategy, commitments to our core personal values, and chapter six looks at communication, the final strategy. Section III looks at life moving forward: Chapter seven pulls it all together, and the resources section lists many useful books and websites.

Great! Let's do this!

GLOSSARY HELP

Are some of the terms here new to you? If so, a detailed glossary of consensual non-monogamy terms can be found on the Loving Without Boundaries website at: lovingwithoutboundaries.com/glossary-key

Cheating — In a relationship, any activity that violates the rules or agreements of that relationship, whether tacit or explicit.

Compersion — A feeling of joy when a partner invests in and takes pleasure from another romantic or sexual relationship.

Metamour — (Literally, meta with; about + amor love): The partner of one's partner, with whom one does not share a direct sexual or loving relationship.

Open Relationship — Any relationship that is not sexually or intimately monogamous.

Polyamory — (Literally, poly many + amor love) The state or practice of maintaining multiple sexual and/or romantic relationships simultaneously, with the full knowledge and consent of all the people involved.

Polycule — A romantic network, or a particular subset of relationships within a romantic network, whose members are closely connected.

Unicorn Hunting — When a heterosexual couple searches for a bisexual woman to be the third in a three-person relationship.

What Is Jealousy Really?

Jealousy is an incredibly complex emotion, and in this chapter, we look at exactly what we mean by jealousy, how it is different from envy, five triggers for jealousy, and three ways people express it.

The Emotion of Jealousy

As human beings, we all experience emotions. Even though it can feel incredibly uncomfortable, jealousy can be a wonderful resource for you — if you are able to re-frame how you view it. Think of the feeling of jealousy as your friend that alerts you to trouble or something in your life that needs your attention. Just as the "check engine" light on your car points out to you that you need to pay attention because something could be wrong, jealousy can let you know that either you, or your relationship, needs some attention. It is a call for you to grab a metaphorical flashlight and look "under the hood" to investigate where those feelings are coming from. Remember, it is your responsibility to look within and take responsibility for your own happiness — not your partner(s) or something outside of yourself, but YOU! That means that it is also your responsibility to find out what the problem is and fix it with whatever tools are at your disposal.

It is also important to keep in mind that jealousy is a tricky little bugger that can take you completely by surprise, smacking you sideways when you least suspect it. The unpredictability of it all can be shocking and make it difficult to think clearly. With some patience with both yourself and your partner(s) however, you can take a deep breath, take stock of the situation, and ponder your next move — hopefully before you act and react impulsively in the heat of the moment. This book will help you tame the destructive impulses, think deeply about jealousy and emotions, and build skills to manage strong feelings.

Imagined Jealousy

It is important to note that all sorts of things can trigger feelings of jealousy — a third party (eg. your partner's partner, otherwise known as your metamour), less time with your love, a wonky situation — something tangible that you can point to and say "that thing over there, that occurrence, this moment we are having is causing me to have some jealous feelings. When we are ready, let's take a closer look at them and discuss them."

However, sometimes people feel jealousy based on assumptions (and we all know when you assume, you make an "ASS" out of "U" and "ME") instead of reality-based facts. Assumption-based jealousy can be a warning sign. Unacknowledged jealousy can be incredibly corrosive to your relationship. If you or your partner(s) are imagining that a partner is cheating, or hiding things, or acting suspiciously, it may be time to seek professional counseling before damaging your relationships further. I would like to state for the record here that seeking outside professional help when you are having a problem does NOT indicate that you are weak or crazy. On the contrary, it means that you are taking care of yourself, your mental health, and your relationships. Let the professionals do what they do best! It can also be extremely useful to have an outside view when wading in to deal with jealousy.

Open Relationship Disclaimer

There are a number of reasons you might read this book. Maybe you are jealous of your sister, friends, or co-workers and wish to deal with the emotion differently. Because my journey to dealing with jealousy started as a way for me to manage my consensually non-monogamous relationships, I focus my conversation here on open or consensually non-monogamous (polyamorous) relationships. Given the simultaneous multiple relationships that may ensue in polyamorous and other open relationships, let's assume that there is in fact a third (or fourth or fifth) person in your relationship structure/polycule, and that you indeed WANT that. Simply put, the information in this book is specially designed for people seeking open relationships who want to understand how to help this configuration succeed for all involved.

If you are in a NON-consensually non-monogamous relationship — meaning that someone is cheating — then the information for you and your partner(s) would be quite different.

Now that we've got that cleared up, let's move on.

Envy Versus Jealousy

Jealousy is a complex emotion, often a combination of fear, anger, sadness, and doubt. Unpacking all that interlocking stuff can take attention, care, and understanding. Let's start with the difference between envy and jealousy as it pertains to relationships.

Envy — WANTING what someone else has

versus

Jealousy — FEAR of potentially LOSING what you have

(That fear can lead to feeling intolerant and hostile toward a [perceived] rival, as well as being fiercely vigilant in guarding a [perceived] possession.)

These are different, and related, emotions. Sometimes you feel them both at the same time, and sometimes you feel one or the other.

WHY DO PEOPLE GET JEALOUS?

Envy, jealousy, and insecurity can rear their frightening heads unpredictably, and often at the worst possible time. To help us get to the heart of the issue, we will take a deeper look at WHY we get jealous. This can help us better manage the situation — in large part so that we don't damage our relationships or connections with people we love. Dealing with jealousy is part of self-care too, because feeling really jealous can feel just awful! Moving through jealousy and getting past it can be a tremendous relief and free up all sorts of energy for other things that feed your life and your soul.

The reasons for jealousy's appearance can fall into (at least) five basic categories.

Five Jealousy Triggers

1) **Possessiveness:** You really want that thing, person, event, feeling, fill-in-the-blank — for yourself and you just don't want to share it with anyone else. In fact, the idea of sharing can feel incredibly threatening.

2) **Low Self-Esteem:** You are afraid that you are not really good enough, and that if your partner sees how wonderful someone else is then they will leave you for that other person who is cooler, more interesting, better-looking, better in bed — just all around better.

3) **Control:** You want your partner to do what you want them to do, in a way you want them to do it, when it works for you. In the more

extreme cases, using jealousy as a way to manipulate and control your partner can become abusive.

The above three are related to feelings of insecurity that we all often feel from to time. These feelings are completely normal, and anyone can choose to improve them over time. Fostering self-care and positive, empowering, and loving feelings towards oneself is a great place to start. More on this later.

4) **Rational Fear:** If you are spending less time with your partner, doing more solo child care, or many other practical and emotional consequences of open relationships, it can be a challenge to work out the details. Sometimes things really are lopsided and need to be rebalanced. Other times cowboys or cowgirls — someone who tries to rope your partner away from the rest of the herd/you and ride off just the two of them — actually are trying to steal your partner.

5) **Vulnerability:** The naked truth is, relationships in general are vulnerable, and people who love are vulnerable to being hurt.

   a) It's a Big Deal
   Losing a close relationship is huge, because you have bonded with this person emotionally, probably developed some degree of practical interdependence, and might have made commitments to each other. You may own cars, houses, and gaming systems together, and you might have kids. Up-ending all of that has significant implications for people's lives.

   b) Threats are Real
   In his review of research on cheating, Grohol (2013) estimates that six percent of heterosexual marital relationships will

experience cheating in any given year, and that number rises to 25% over the course of the relationship. Others who include different kinds of relationships (dating, cohabitation, online interactions, same-sex relationships, etc.) have much higher estimates of 23% of men and 15% of women engaging in some kind of cheating behavior in a given year (Martins et al., 2016). Open relationships are no guarantee to keep relationships safe from cheating, either. Cheaters or cowgirls/boys aren't necessarily all mean-spirited or intending to ruin your life. Most of the time, they think your partner rocks (like you do) and want that person all to themselves.

THREE REACTIONS

Not only is jealousy triggered by a variety of things in our social environments, it also comes out in a variety of ways. Jealousy can be disruptive or constructive, or some mix of those. Sometimes people don't get jealous at all but instead react with compersion, or happiness that their partner(s) are happy with someone else.

Disruptive Jealousy

Sometimes jealousy can be disruptive, such as when someone in an established relationship views another person as an unwanted rival. Disruptive jealousy can express as a desire to punish the partner for interacting with the external person, or even active disruption of their relationship using tactics such as by calling the new person and telling them to bugger off, using "veto power" to try to remove them, or calling one's partner during dates to intentionally interrupt.

So in short, examples of disruptive jealousy are:
1) **Viewing the new person as an unwanted rival and taking action to remove them.**
2) **Punishing a partner for interacting with their new love interest.**

Do Not Despair

All of this gloomy talk of pain, control, and disruption may have you feeling pretty crappy just about now, but take heart! There are other ways to react to jealousy and/or jealousy provoking situations. We have all grown up in cultures that condition us to think monogamy is the only right way to be, and unlearning that takes some time and attention. While you can expect to have some monogamous left-overs to clear out of your relationship refrigerator, you can also shop for some exciting new condiments in the section below. Instead of the spoiled half and half of manipulation and disruption, reach for the exciting new zest of constructive jealousy and compersion!

Constructive Jealousy

Sometimes when you are feeling jealousy, you just need to ride it out and let it happen. In such cases, you can learn to express jealousy in a way that does not punish your partner or interfere with your partner's relationships with other people. Learning to feel the jealousy and allow it to pass can be a challenge, and I talk about that later in the book. For this first chapter, it is enough to say that learning how to calm yourself down and feel better is a great overall life skill. Learning to tolerate jealousy can help you flex emotional muscles that you didn't even know you had. Yay!

Compersion?!

In a culture based on monogamy, we are conditioned to react with jealousy because we are supposed to have the one, the only, the true and sole soul-mate. Anything outside of that is unsettling and even threatening, so the idea of being happy seeing your partner being happy with someone else can take some getting used to. The opposite of jealousy, compersion is a feeling of happiness that your partner has found joy with someone else. You may or may not have experienced compersion. Good on you if you do. Don't worry if you don't (as long as you stay constructive). It is something you can cultivate over time, if you choose.

CHAPTER I

Pre-Game Prep: Positive Mindset

"A pessimist sees the difficulty in every opportunity; an optimist sees the opportunity in every difficulty."

— Sir Winston Churchill

There is an old joke about a tourist visiting New York who sees a man on the street carrying a violin. Stopping the violinist, the tourist asks how to get to Carnegie Hall. The violinist responds "Practice, practice, practice!"

Obviously, we all know that when we practice something we get better at it. Learning new skills can be difficult or frustrating, and developing true mastery of new abilities can take time. While we expect to have to spend some time learning to swim or program computers, it can be more challenging to extend that same patience to learning new relationship skills. Hang in there — spending the time and effort now can provide some fantastic rewards in the future.

In their incredibly useful book, *Emotional Blackmail*, Susan Forward and Donna Frazier (1997) affirm that:

"When it comes to making important changes in our lives, we often expect results overnight. The unavoidable truth is that learning new skills takes practice, and it may be awhile before you're comfortable using them. Just as we have to walk around in a new pair of shoes before they really fit, we have to break in a new behavior. You probably won't see immediate changes in your life the first day you make the commitment — but you will see them soon. Remember, commitment is a promise to yourself, and it's one well worth keeping."

You should expect to put some time and energy into practicing these skills, and give yourself a break while you are at it. If you practice using these strategies, you will almost certainly experience growing pains. But take heart — it may seem hard now, but you will get better at this as you practice and grow. These skills will become more familiar and easier over time.

The secret to overnight success is daily positivity and daily action. Each small success helps create more!

FIRST MISSION — CREATING A POSITIVE MINDSET

Before you think about constructively dealing with jealousy, there are some items we should consider first. Every day for the next week or more, I'd like you to set aside some private time to work with three simple exercises to help enhance your success: 1) a contract, 2) a power statement, and 3) a set of self-affirming phrases/empowering beliefs.

You'll need as little as 15 minutes a day. During this time, I'd like you to turn off the phone, remove yourself from interruptions, and focus on you. I know many of you probably find that you have limited private time (eg. bathtub, commute time, eating lunch at your desk). That is absolutely fine. You can do this practice anywhere you want in 15 minutes!

Mindset Shift One: Contract

▶ WHAT IS ACHIEVABLE IN YOUR LIFE IS BASED UPON THE BELIEFS YOU GIVE TO YOURSELF. CHOOSE YOUR BELIEFS WISELY! ◀

The first thing I'd like you to do for yourself is to create and sign a contract that lists a number of promises I'd like you to make to yourself — ground rules if you will for this process. You may have serious doubts at this point about your ability to keep promises like these, especially if you've tried unsuccessfully in the past to handle your jealousy productively and with grace. Now is the time to put the past aside right now, and begin to take a new set of steps based on a fresh understanding and additional skills.

You might find that you get the best results from hand-writing this contract on a sheet of paper, possibly in a notebook you devote to the exercises I'll be teaching you. It can also be a good idea to record your observations and feelings as we go. Whatever method you choose, please read the contract aloud to yourself every day this week. Also, feel free to amend this contract to fit your own situation.

"Live your happiest life by tapping into choice, not habit, in your words and actions."

— Karen Salmansohn

Contract With Myself

I, _____, recognize myself as an adult with options and choices, and I commit myself to the process of actively working with jealousy within my relationships in constructive ways. In order to reach that goal, I make the following promises:

- I promise myself that I will resist comparison to others, or the desire to manipulate or punish others. I take control over my own decisions, and refuse to allow those emotions to control my actions in my relationships.
- I promise myself that I will learn the strategies in this book and that I will put them into practice in my life.
- I promise myself that I will give this my absolute best effort and learn to grow through these emotions. If I make mistakes, stumble, or fall into old patterns, I will keep on trying. Even if it is hard, I will try again.
- I promise to take good care of myself during this process.
- I promise that I will acknowledge myself for taking positive steps, even the small ones.

_____ Signature

_____Date

Mindset Shift Two: Power Statement

Next, I'd like you to learn and practice saying a power statement, one short sentence that you can use to keep yourself grounded when the emotion of jealousy turns up the heat.

⪢ Power statement: I can stand it. ⪡

Those four words may look insignificant, but when used correctly, they can become one of your most powerful tools for handling jealousy. These four powerful words are so effective because they help counter the cultural conditioning that we are powerless to handle jealousy constructively. In a culture that sees jealousy as an irresistible force, it is no surprise that many of us suffer with the idea that we can't stand the pressure or the emotions coursing through our bodies. Some examples of destructive self-talk that pushes us to feel powerless:

- I can't stand to feel this (emotion of jealousy).
- I can't stand to see them together.
- I can't stand when he/she/they are on a date.
- I can't stand my anxiety.
- I can't stand it when they kiss/cuddle.
- I can't stand knowing I'm not the only one.

When we constantly make statements like these to ourselves, it reinforces the idea that we truly cannot tolerate the situation. If you really believe you can't stand it, you'll only be able to see one course of action. You'll give in to a knee-jerk freak out reaction, scream, try to manipulate the situation, and end up damaging your relationships. With this new statement "I CAN stand it," you are effectively changing your current belief system little by little. Though you may not believe it now, you are a lot stronger than you think! You CAN stand the feeling and the pressure or anxiety you may experience, and your first step is to replace any belief that tells you otherwise.

Repeating "I CAN stand it" will begin putting a new message into your conscious and unconscious mind. For this week, every time you think about taking steps to handle jealousy as it courses through your body and start to feel frightened, upset or discouraged, take a moment to repeat this statement to yourself. Breathe deeply, exhale completely and repeat "I can stand it." Do this at least 10 times aloud. As Yoda would say "Do not 'try' — DO!"

You can DO this! You may be timid with it at first, and not very convincing, but stay with it. You'll start to believe yourself. Is this process mechanical? Yes. Does it feel foreign? Yes, it might. But remember that your old responses may not have worked well or been constructive. I assure you that repeating "I can stand it" to yourself does work.

Mindset Shift Three: Empowering Beliefs

"Being happy isn't about what you have.
It's about the thoughts you have."

— Karen Salmansohn

Now, using the same basic concept of replacing old beliefs with new ones, I'd like to help you develop a set of self-affirming phrases that will help to calm you, make you feel stronger, and embolden you to act constructively, rather than destructively. First, let's take a look at a set of statements that describe the typical feelings and behavior of someone experiencing a full-tilt attack of jealousy. Most, or even all, of the statements may be true for you — not in all of your relationships, but when you face strong feelings of jealousy.

When dealing with jealousy, do you do any of the following?

___ I tell myself that screaming, making demands, and lashing out is my right.
___ I tell myself that I am "wrong" for feeling jealous.
___ I tell myself that my needs and desires are wrong.
___ I tell myself that talking about it is not worth the battle.
___ I tell myself that my unmet needs or violated values do not matter.
___ I say and do nothing now because I'll take a stand for my needs and wants later.
___ I don't stand up for myself.
___ I do things to please other people and get confused about what I want.
___ I tell myself that I must control my partner(s) and their actions, needs and wants.
___ I villainize my metamour (my partner's other partner) by telling myself that person is wrong, evil, or bad.
___ I blame my partner(s) and their actions for my feelings and thoughts.
___ I criticize and judge other people in my circle, making them wrong and me right.
___ Experiencing jealousy will crush me, and I can't survive it.
___ My partner is mine and I take ownership of this person in my life.

These statements sound pretty weak, don't they? If you identify with some of these statements, there is no need to be embarrassed. Until a few years ago, some of the statements would have been true for me too in certain relationships or situations — and they're true for many people just like you! Jealousy is a very common emotion, and we're all in this together. Remember, this takes practice, patience, and kindness for yourself and your partner(s).

Pay attention to how the statements you've checked make you feel, and use the following list to help you pinpoint the full range of feelings that go along with this thought process and behaviors. Notice or circle the words that apply to you, and add any other feelings you're aware of that I haven't listed.

Ask yourself:
"How do I feel when I think these thoughts and/or act this way?"

Embarrassed	Sad
Hurt	Powerless
Ashamed	Self-pitying
Angry	Helpless
Cunning	Distracted
Weak	Vindictive
Depressed	Agitated
Frustrated	Scared
Emotionally numb	Resentful
Powerful	Victimized

If you circled angry, I wouldn't be surprise if you were not only perhaps angry at a partner or metamour, but also angry at yourself, and even angry at me for reminding you of certain aspects of your behavior that you'd rather forget. Use this discomfort — it's letting you know what aspects of your behavior and thought process need attention.

> *"Be careful not to do something permanently stupid because you are angry, stressed, scared, tired, or hungry."*
> — KAREN SALMANSOHN

Now take your original list of old statements, and change each item you've check to its new opposite. For example:

Old: I tell myself that screaming, making demands, and lashing out is my right.
New: I take responsibility for my feelings, calm myself down before speaking to loved ones, and make requests (not demands).

Old: I tell myself that my needs and desires are wrong.
New: I ask for what I want, even when it's uncomfortable or makes me feel vulnerable.

Old: I do things to please other people and get confused about what I want.
New: I do things to please myself as well as others, and I am clear about what I want.

Old: I tell myself that I must control my partner and his/her/their actions, needs and wants.
New: I CAN and WILL let go of the outcome of a situation.

Old: My partner is mine and I take ownership of this person in my life.
New: I know and recognize that I don't "own" my partner — I am responsible for me, my health, and my happiness only.

Old: I blame my partner and his/her/their actions for my feelings and thoughts.
New: I control how and what I feel.

Old: Experiencing jealousy will crush me and I can't survive it.
New: I can accomplish anything I set my mind to, and I CAN stand experiencing the feeling of jealousy. I realize it is a normal, human emotion.

You can also put your original behavior statements in the past tense by saying, "I used to [statement], but I don't do that anymore." For example, "I used to tell myself that I own my partner, but I don't do that anymore."

Try both approaches and see which feels best to you. Then repeat these new positive statements aloud as if they described you. I know they are not true right now, but they'll give you a sense of what it will feel like to be free of behaviors driven by anger, rage and jealousy. Putting these statements in the past tense or restating them in a positive way helps drain power from them and return it to you! How awesome is that?

Some of my clients have found this exercise to be especially effective when they stand up and state the new beliefs aloud using emphasis and arm or facial gestures. Making the statements more physical like that will give you a chance to literally feel in your bones your new thoughts and actions in an affirmative way. You may feel silly or awkward and giggle the first few times, but you will get used to it and it will come to feel more natural over time.

Think about how you would feel if you were to act in this new way based on these empowering beliefs. Use the following list to help you describe those feelings.

Strong	Courageous
Elated	Hopeful
Self-affirming	Serene
Proud	Peaceful
Triumphant	Abundant
Powerful	Fearless
Confident	Brave
Excited	Loving
Capable	Resilient

These adjectives will help you visualize yourself successfully handling jealous feelings. Change starts with a vision, and it's important to give yourself a clear mental picture of what you are trying to achieve. Then as we work, you can energize your vision with action and move steadily toward your goal. You may want to write or repeat a statement that expresses this vision, such as:

"I can effectively and constructively handle any jealous feelings or thoughts, and feel strong, confident, proud, and elated."

SUMMARY OF BEFORE-YOU-GET-STARTED PREPARATION EXERCISES

Way to go! You now have a contract, a power statement or two, and some empowering new beliefs. After a week of working by yourself with these three exercises, you should be feeling more centered and ready to start dealing directly with your current situation. Let yourself take the time to do the preparatory exercises, no matter how eager you are to get going. You have plenty of time — the human emotion of jealousy and the triggers that prompt it for you aren't going anywhere. You already are far ahead of the "jealousy game" by taking these preliminary steps to empower your mind and heart to live and love compassionately and constructively. Go you!

CHAPTER 2

Jealousy Game Plan: S.O.S.

> *"The bigger your life challenges,
> the bigger your opportunity for growth."*
> — Karen Salmansohn

In the heat of the moment, it can be challenging to stay with newly acquired skills instead of going back to old habits that don't serve us. Why? Because the old ways feel familiar and comfortable, even though the outcome of our actions can be detrimental to us. What you need during those times of stress is something easy to remember, a go-to acronym and plan to help you when emotions are flaring up threatening to hijack your brain and good sense.

SECOND MISSION — CREATE A WINNING GAME PLAN SENDING UP AN S.O.S.

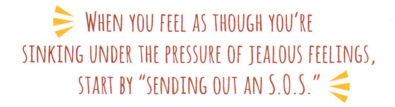

Thank you, Sting.

You don't need to know Morse code, have flares ready, or understand the hand-held system of flags to communicate. Instead, remember this convenient shorthand for the first three steps in this behavior change process.

S.O.S.: Stop. Observe. Strategize.

We'll cover the first two steps in this chapter and explore tools and strategies in the chapters that follow. Please don't skip any steps here — building your chosen strategies on a strong and solid foundation is essential and will contribute greatly to your success and ultimate happiness. Who doesn't want that? Let's do this!

STEP ONE: STOP

This may seem counterintuitive, but you read that right. When you feel jealousy starting to take over and adrenaline coursing through your veins, I want you to simply STOP — do and say nothing. It took me a while to realize that this was the key to success to helping reduce drama and misery in my life related to succumbing to knee-jerk reactions that can feel so seductive in the moment. How do I know? Because of course I also did the opposite … and much drama and misery ensued! "Bad Kitty, bop yourself on the head with a newspaper!"

When you first read it here, doing nothing may sound easy. In truth, it can be quite challenging, however, especially when your feelings are very intense and it feels compelling to take immediate action. It's important to brace yourself and prepare as much as possible before those overwhelming feelings crop up. You'll perhaps feel awkward at first. That's OK and understandable. Go ahead and feel awkward — it's just an uncomfortable feeling and nothing more — and keep going.

Learning to tolerate discomfort in the service of healthy change is one of the most difficult things any of us must do. In the past, discomfort may have been a prelude to lashing out, panicking, or having a full-on freak out. Now that you are challenging all that, you're probably going to feel uneasy and unsteady. It's OK to feel uncertain and anxious as you regain your footing. Things are starting to shift internally and externally, and I want to reassure you that it's perfectly natural to feel shaky when that's happening. Don't let discomfort throw you off course though. Remember that's it's just discomfort, not actual damaging or lethal physical pain. Big difference! Remember:

In *Emotional Blackmail* (1997), Forward and Frazier explain that:

"Internal discomfort is one of the major impediments to change, and we're so used to responding to it as though it were a fire to be put out that many of us haven't learned to live with it in the natural amounts that accompany change. We push it away, extinguish it, treat it as though it has no place in our lives — and by doing so, we eliminate some of our most effective options. **Most of us are so reluctant to examine our discomfort that we often misinterpret what it's trying to tell us by reacting to its presence blindly instead of asking what it means.**"

So how do you do nothing? In such an action-oriented culture, it can be hard to envision how to do nothing. The first thing you need to do is give yourself time to think — away from the trigger so that you don't do something that you might regret to alleviate your discomfort. In some cases, you can take a moment for yourself. I'm not talking about turning your heel and oddly (and possibly rudely) leaving the other person without explanation. I'm talking about excusing yourself and going to another room where you can be quiet for a few minutes. To do this, you'll need to learn some time-buying phrases that will slow things down. Below I've listed some suggestions for your first response to whatever the situation happens to be:

- I'll be right back.
- I need a drink of water/to re-fresh my drink.
- I need to use the restroom — be back shortly.

Or if you're feeling really anxious, how about:
- I need a drink of water, and I need to use the restroom.

If direct honesty in that specific moment is acceptable, you can try:
- This is hard.
- I need to take time to sort this out / calm down / get some perspective.

It can also be helpful to say:
- I value this relationship. I'll be right back.
- ... to give the other person reassurance that you aren't turning away.

Buying yourself some time gives you a chance to experience your own thoughts, remember your priorities, and explore your feelings. Remember that you have this new lifeline to hold onto — your time-buying statements that we'll discover together. You may feel like a broken record by the time you're through repeating them, but keep going and give them a chance to work at giving you space to calm down and think straight.

By the way, you can do this at home, in a restaurant, at the office, on an airplane — just about anywhere. Putting some physical distance between you and the jealousy trigger can take a lot of urgency out of your need to "do something" and possibly act out, and give you some all-important emotional distance as well.

By "gaining some emotional distance", I mean turning down the flame and allowing your feelings to cool. When confronted with a jealousy triggering situation, your feelings may be so intense and full of frantic energy that you can't think, reason, consider options, or make good choices. The loud symphony of feelings can seem deafening and overwhelming. You're in a state of pure emotional reactivity, and you need to move into a more cognitive, detached mode. We'll go into this more in the next chapter with our first strategy: Defusion. Either way taking a few moments to quiet yourself will do that for you. Calm yourself, repeat "I can stand it," and buy yourself some time.

STEP TWO: OBSERVE

Great! You've been able to create the space you need to let your frenzied emotions dial back in an effort to think more clearly. Most excellent! Now you are more prepared and centered enough to dive into the second step — OBSERVE. Now that you have bought yourself some time (Great job!), you're positioned to become an observer of yourself, the other people, and the situation.

Use Visualization

Occasionally using a technique like visualization can help take us to another more empowering place. In this case, we'll use visualization to literally help us become an observer of our lives, relationships, and each unique situation.

To help you do this, I'd like you to experiment with this visualization exercise. I suggest this one because it is a tried and true exercise that works for me and others, but you should definitely feel free to modify it or use a similar visualization exercise that works better for you.

Observation Tower Exercise

In *Emotional Blackmail* (1997), Forward and Frazier suggest the following exercise:

"Envision a glass elevator on the ground floor of a 50-story observation tower. I'd like you to picture yourself inside the elevator as the car slowly starts to move up. As you look out on the lower floors, it's difficult to see anything because of a swirling ground fog. Occasionally the fog breaks and you can make out the outlines of objects and people, but they're vague and fuzzy, appearing and disappearing. This is the realm of pure emotions, the gut feelings that [jealousy can] churn up in us.

The elevator car keeps moving up, and as it does, you leave the fog behind and begin to see a wider landscape. By the time you reach the top, you have a panoramic view, and you can see that the fog that you thought covered everything is confined to the valley at the base of the tower. What seemed all-encompassing was just a tiny patch, a small part of the picture. The elevator has reached a different plane, a place of reason, perception, and objectivity. Step out of the car onto the observation platform. Enjoy the quiet and the clarity. Remember that you always have access to this place."

Traveling up from the gut level to the head is useful when you're lost in the sea of feelings of jealousy. It is all too easy to get caught up in the dreaded fearful feelings of "loss, less, or never" while our perceptions become fragmented or distorted. To be clear here, I'm not asking you to detach from your feelings — I'm simply suggesting that you add perception and reason to the mix so that you're not driven SOLELY by feeling. Both the intellect and our emotions contain a great deal of information, and we're looking to create an exchange between the two. The goal is to be able to think and feel at the same time, rather than just thrashing around in the emotions alone. When jealousy heats up, we need the cool perspective of the Observation Tower.

What's Really Happening/Happened?

So often much of our fear of "loss, less, or never" comes from the stories we tell ourselves about what is happening, or what one of my heroes Brené Brown often calls the "Shitty First Draft" (SFD) that she highlights in her amazing book, *Rising Strong* (2015). We concoct numerous worst-case scenarios that scare the living daylights out of us, including imagining lots of frightening feelings and outcomes! Talk about creating a self-sabotaging freak out! Even worse, we have no idea if these stories are even true!

Why on Earth do we do this to ourselves? Partly because we are human, and as humans we like to create stories to explain things to ourselves. Unfortunately, sometimes we craft these stories in such a counter-productive, un-empowering, and scary way that we end up diminishing our partners without even realizing what we are doing. In order to counteract that, let's stick to the facts only — no stories!

External (events): Just the facts, Jack.

Here we focus on the situation that triggers jealousy, stepping into the role of observer who has come to report on what they see. "Just the facts, Jack" is the phrase of the day. Your feelings will still be there, but turn your attention away from them and let your mind review the situation for just what it actually is. Ask yourself: "What just happened?" Writing down the answers to the questions that follow can be especially useful. Taking information out of your head and putting it on paper also helps you gain emotional distance to look at it in the external world. Alternately, you can do this entirely in your head. Either way, answering these questions can provide a lot of clarity for you.

Take a moment to step back and look at the facts:

- What has actually transpired?
- Who were the players?
- What kind of body language and tone of voice did the players use?
- What physical sensations did you notice in your body?
- What are your current pre-existing agreements? Did all of the players know about these agreements before this happened?
This is important, because others can't respect our boundaries that they do not explicitly know about! We can't hold partners accountable for unspoken agreements or expectations.

Next, look at your own reactions to the situation.

Internal (mind): What are you thinking?
Write down what's going through your mind, paying special attention to thoughts that repeat or keep intruding. They will give you valuable insights into the beliefs that you have formed over the years. Among the common beliefs I see in jealousy moments are:

- Getting rejected is the worst thing that could happen to me, and this absolutely IS rejection.
- This person is disrespecting me/violating my boundaries — no question.
- They don't love me anymore.
- I cannot stand this.
- That other person (my metamour) is better/stronger/sexier/prettier than me.
- My partner no longer needs me because they have this/these other people.

Which of these statements seem true to you? Which do you identify with the most? Ask yourself: Where did I learn this, and how long have I believed it? Take note and reflect on what answers come back to you.

None of these beliefs may actually be true, yet we cling to them in moments of fear and doubt. It's important to identify our beliefs about ourselves as they come up in the face of jealousy triggers because beliefs are the precursor to feelings. Feelings aren't the fleeting, independent forces we think they are. Rather, feelings are almost always a response to what we think. Nearly every anxious, sad, fearful, or upsetting feeling we have in response to a jealousy trigger follows a negative or erroneous belief about our own adequacy, lovability, and desirableness to others. When it comes to jealousy, these beliefs are the drivers of our feelings.

The Bottom Line: To change self-defeating behavior patterns, we must start with the root element — our beliefs.

Uncovering your deep beliefs can help you learn why you feel the way you do. Once you've been able to do that, you'll begin to see how these beliefs and feelings become the catalyst for self-sabotaging behaviors which can, unfortunately, damage your otherwise good/great relationship.

Internal (heart): How are you feeling?

Let's turn the focus inward to our emotions. What do you feel as you replay the event in your mind's eye? Write down as many feelings as you are aware of. Take note that sometimes we use words that aren't really feelings but are actually thoughts instead. You can begin by using the following list of feelings:

Angry	Hurt
Irritated	Frustrated
Anxious	Doomed
Trapped	Resentful

Threatened	Disappointed
Insecure	Scared
Inadequate	Stuck
Unlovable / Rejected	Sad
Overwhelmed	Depressed

Remember that we can think of our feelings as check engine lights to help let us know when we need to pay attention to something. This check-in is the equivalent of taking your emotional pulse. And though it's simple, it's an important diagnostic tool — just like the check engine light for your car. To help stay on the feeling-track only, keep in mind that a feeling is an emotional state that can be expressed in one, or at most two words. The moment you say "I feel like…" Or "I feel that…", you're describing what you think or believe, not an actual feeling. Because we're trying to differentiate between thoughts and feelings so that you can understand the relationships between them, it's important to be clear on the distinctions.

For example: "I feel that my lover likes him/her/them better" is a thought. To get to the feeling, you can say, "I believe that my lover likes him/her/them better, and I feel sad."

Now check in with your body in relation to your feelings.

As you look at your list, identify where you feel these feelings physically. Burning in your cheeks? Are they churning in your stomach? Knotting in your throat? Notice how your body reacts to your feelings.

It's interesting to realize that often our bodies will often tell us a truth that our minds keep hidden. We may say we're not feeling particularly anxious — and then notice that we're drenched with perspiration. "No, no, nothing is wrong — so why is my stomach in knots?" This used to happen to me before I would perform on stage in my rock band on "gig" days. In my mind, I thought I was completely calm, not in the least bit nervous. But my body illustrated the truth as I kept going to the restroom over and over all day long until I took the stage. Yep that's the honest and rather hilarious truth — I would get the shits! My body's response to the day's events cut through my denial and rationalization, and your body won't lie to you either.

A powerful way to observe your feelings is to get curious about them, meaning approach noticing them from a place of curiosity. You can try thinking... "Hmmmm, isn't that interesting that whenever I see _____, I feel _____." This objectivity helps put you in a more thoughtful mode and helps to insulate you from over-reaction, self-criticism, and making erroneous interpretations (that "Shitty First Draft" that we spoke of earlier).

SUMMARY OF JEALOUSY GAME PLAN: S.O.S.

You now have an easy-to-remember game plan to cling to readily when you find yourself in the throes of jealous feelings: Our S.O.S. game plan of Stop, Observe, Strategize. In this chapter, we reviewed how to STOP to gain some valuable time and perspective while we let our emotions cool down. This pausing step helps you to be able to think more clearly and rationally to then go to Step Two: OBSERVE what actually happened rather than the story that you are telling yourself based on your thoughts and beliefs around the situation. Then, observe the feelings that come up based on those beliefs.

In the next section, I'll give you the tools to turn this preparation and knowledge into effective strategies that will dramatically alter the outcome of your reactions to a jealousy triggering situation to be more constructive than your previous reactions that were potentially destructive to you and your relationships. Wouldn't that be nice?

Ready? Let's do this!

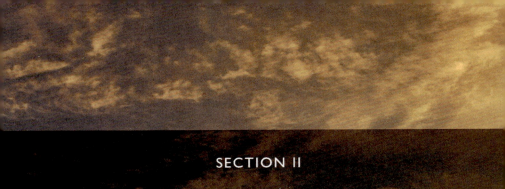

SECTION II
STRATEGIES FOR DEALING WITH JEALOUSY

CHAPTER 3

Strategy One: Defusion

"We have thoughts, feelings, and emotions, but we are not our thoughts, feelings, or emotions."

— Frances Vaughn

The first section of this book defined jealousy and set the stage for our discussion. This second section presents the four-step Constructive Jealousy Framework: Defusion, Compassion, Commitment to Personal Values, and Communication. Based on Kelly Cookson's teachings and used here with his permission, the Constructive Jealousy Framework is a method and teaching program meant to guide you to channel your energy and jealous feelings towards a productive, empowering, and positive outcome. My hope for you is that this framework offers you an alternative to the possibly destructive outcomes to your relationship and well-being that you may have experienced in the past, and instead allows you to flourish in love and security.

We come up against moments in our lives where fear prevails. If we are not aware that we are afraid, this may manifest as anxiety. A wise person once told me that, "anxiety is simply emotions that you've not yet identified or allowed yourself to feel." I try to think of this anytime I feel myself becoming afraid of what is ahead (the future...the unknown). I find that when I take a moment to be with myself and what I am feeling, my fears begin to lose their power.

I have realized that many of the fears that creep up for me are related to the unknown or to expectations of how I think things should be or predictions that I make. When I live in a place of fear, my mind feels jumbled/foggy and I find I don't fully live in the moment. However, when we take time to ground and center ourselves, we can tap into how we are truly feeling. Once we can identify the feelings, we then have something to work with when it comes time to "let go." I find that when I face my fears head on, I am presented with ample opportunity for growth. I end up learning something new about myself, discovering a new layer of what I am capable of. Fear is an excellent opportunity to discover something new about yourself.

First, however, we need to learn to detach from our fear and expectations, so that we can get back to living in the moment and acting constructively. Our first strategy helps us do just that.

DEFUSION

Purpose: See thoughts and feelings as what they are, not as what they say to us they are.

When to use: When personal events are functioning as barriers due to FEAR (False Expectations Appearing Real)

Defusion is the opposite of fusion. In this context, fusion means melding with our thoughts as if they are completely "true," thus then we act as if they are commands. Defusion — also known as Cognitive Defusion or Deliteralization — is practicing the opposite — observing and then questioning our thoughts and detaching from them when possible.

When we practice defusion, we can learn to see thoughts as what they truly are, rather than what our thoughts tell us they are. We can learn the difference between "true" and "truth." As people living consciously, it can be empowering to question everything — including our own thoughts. This is especially important when those thoughts are not serving us. Defusion is not about resisting our emotions; it's about feeling them completely and yet not turning our choices and our power over to them.

In the tenacious grip of jealousy, it can be all too easy to feel like we are powerless against it. As part of the human condition, we all experience unpleasant or painful emotions from time to time. These feelings do not need to devastate our lives. Our emotions and feelings are just that — feelings! Don't make them more than they are.

Fear Disguised as Jealousy

Because jealousy can teach us many things about ourselves, we can choose to view it as a gift. In many cases, the origins of jealousy can be traced back to FEAR over experiencing one of three things: Loss, Less, or Never. Fear of loss of a partner, fear of less time/devotion/attention from a partner, never seeing our partner again, or never having them look at us that same special way again... and on and on it goes, like a hamster wheel.

Sometimes when we feel an emotion that is new or uncomfortable, our natural response is fear and we try to run away from it — like it's a sabretooth tiger chasing us. Our focus can narrow down to that one thing that is terrifying us so much that we can't see anything else, as if we were wearing blinders. When that happens, we can become skittish, unpredictable, and cut off from what's happening around us. But if we could lightly touch the threat — in this case, the feeling of jealousy or even fear of jealousy — we can realize that we can let the emotion pass through us as we "touch" it, eventually settle down, and see that we are just fine. It was not a sabretooth tiger chasing us, it was simply an emotion.

Fear is a natural and normal feeling for humans, and it can come up frequently in intimate relationships. By using these techniques, we can learn to touch the fear to help take some of the difficult charge out of it.

When fear, jealousy, anxiety, or anger bubble up and seem to take over our minds, we can become preoccupied by the feelings and focused on getting rid of them. We tend to treat internal discomfort as if it is the same as a real threat in the external world. In the grip of painful emotions, it can be difficult to focus on what is happening around us. We tend to ignore the suggestions of our wiser selves and make foolish or impulsive decisions.

What if we could learn how to respond differently to painful emotions? What if we could lightly touch the feelings that scare us? With time and practice, we might find that — although they seem very threatening — emotions can't actually harm us. Like all new skills, it is good to start small with less challenging emotions. Touch them gently by getting curious about them and imagining yourself expanding to make room for them.

> **If we repeatedly practice the skill of turning toward emotional discomfort with curiosity, something important happens.**

When fear, jealousy, or anger inevitably turn up, instead of freaking out and being controlled by our emotions, we can accept our feelings as signs that we are human and that we care. Rather than allowing our fear and angst to take control, we can take actions based on our values and what options the situation affords. Over time, these wiser choices will help us to flourish in ALL of our relationships.

Be a warrior, not a worrier.

DEFUSION TECHNIQUES

Here I will share with you some valuable techniques that you can use to gently train your mind and your thoughts to work for you — not against you. Experiment with each technique to see which ones work best for you.

1) **Thank Your Brain** — Tell yourself: "Thank you brain for trying to protect me by warning me of a possible danger. But I know there is no life-threatening danger and I can make my own decision. You may be quiet now. Stand down."

2) **Treat Your Brain as Separate Entity** — You can treat your brain as an external event, almost as a separate person. Your brain is not you, it's just your brain which is one piece of you — not ALL of you. You are also your heart, your entire body, your soul, your spirit. You have the choice at any time to use all of these parts of yourself to make decisions about your behavior, actions, thoughts, and even your feelings.

3) **Label Thoughts** — If you think "I'm a loser and my partner doesn't love me," you can just observe that thought. Instead of getting hung up and wrapped in a freaked out knot of terror, you defuse from it and distance yourself from negative thoughts like that. Instead, you can say "There's that silly 'loser' thought again." Identifying it

as a silly and negative thought makes it easier to detach from that thought and let it go. It also helps take the charge or the heat out of it to help make it more tolerable. Remember: You CAN stand it!

4) **Silliness and Songs** — Use silly voices or turn these scary thoughts into song and thus make it less serious or threatening and minimize the power. Feel free to get creative and have fun!

5) **Name Your Story** — What's the story you are telling yourself? Give it a name, something like "Jealousy Story A." You can get creative with this and use humor again to help take some of the charge out of the story or your "Shitty First Draft" interpretation about what is going on. A creative name such as a silly "My Metamour is an Evil Three-Headed Ogre" story name reminds us that our story is not actually true, but is instead a figment of our vivid imagination.

6) **Create and Name Your Jealousy Gremlin** — To help externalize your jealousy gremlin and make an effort to tame it, get creative by using a stuffed animal, toy, artwork, or create your own imaginative item to represent your jealousy gremlin. In essence, we are dragging that gremlin out into the light to lessen its power. Give it an interesting or funny name, like "Mr. Green Meanie Beanie." When jealousy flares up, you can talk to it kindly (after all, it is a part of wonderful you!), but assertively and firmly. Say "Thank you, Gremlin, for trying to look out for me and protect me. But I've got it from here. Please be quiet and go back in your cave now."

7) **Thoughts Can't Hurt** — Remember your thoughts can't actually hurt you like a gun. They are simply thoughts! You can ignore them or change them. Remember that YOU are in control of the bus of your life, not your thoughts. Prove it to yourself.

Example: Put your hand on your knee. Think the thought that "I can't raise my hand." Then raise your hand. There — you just proved to yourself that your thoughts can't control you :) Simple yet powerful! You are NOT your thoughts!

8) **Leaves on a Stream** — Imagine your thought perched on a leaf in a stream and is floating away from you. This helps you visualize letting go of that thought and having it drift out of your consciousness, leaving room for more empowering thoughts that better serve you.

DEFUSION SKILL GOAL

Gain psychological space from your thoughts so you don't act on them, potentially causing conflict by acting impulsively. Impulsive action can be damaging to relationships, and then no one wins!

SUMMARY OF DEFUSION SKILL

The next time you feel yourself having a jealousy freak out, take a deep breath and see if you could, just for a moment, experience your feelings with an attitude of kindness and curiosity. It might just change everything! With time and practice, you can learn to use some of these skills we are discussing here to get space from your thoughts, and realize that your thoughts don't control you.

In this way, you can learn to let go of your struggle against feelings of jealousy and pain, assess your values (coming up in chapter five), and then commit to acting in ways that further those values.

CHAPTER 4

Strategy Two: Compassion

> *"Between stimulus and response, there is a space. In that space lies our freedom and our power to choose our response. In our response lies our growth and our happiness."*
>
> — Viktor Frankl

What if I told you that you could increase the quality of your relationships by using a simple tool to foster your own capacity for love, kindness and compassion?

You'd want it right? Well, I'm going to give you that tool right now.

COMPASSION (MEDITATION)

Compassion Meditation to Boost Loving-Kindness

Compassion helps us mend relationships and move forward while fostering emotional intelligence and well-being. What is "emotional intelligence"?

Emotional Intelligence (EI) — The ability to monitor one's own and other's feelings and emotions, to discriminate among them, and use this information to guide one's thinking and actions (Van Dyne et al., 2012). In other words, Emotional Intelligence is a learned skill. Practicing compassion meditation and mindfulness can help us get to greater levels of EI. So what exactly is mindfulness?

Mindfulness — "Settling the mind to be focused and fully engaged in the present." — Vasco Gaspar

Cultivating mindfulness helps us to manage our fear responses, such as the fear we experience in the grips of a jealousy triggering situation or thought.

You too can enjoy the benefits of emotional intelligence and loving-kindness with a guided meditation. This type of mediation comes from the tenets of Buddhism, but you don't have to be a practicing Buddhist to reap the rewards of this fantastic tool! This kind of meditation increases both compassion and resilience to overcoming challenging situations.

Speaking from experiences in my own life, I first learned about compassion mediation from a therapist I was seeing during a particularly challenging period of my life. I was still grieving my father's death and all too soon it appeared that my mother was also knocking at death's door. This all transpired after my husband and I found out we were infertile and had suffered failed IVF treatment. I felt broken, defeated, lost, and mad at the world. Compassion meditation was one of the tools that I used to slowly climb out of the abyss that I found myself in, putting myself back together piece by piece. I learned compassion not only for myself, but also for others in my life who meant well, but didn't know how to support me through that incredibly difficult period. I even found compassion for the larger world around me. It was transformative!

Later I used compassion meditation as I was diving head first into my exciting and challenging polyamorous journey. I grew up learning that monogamy was the only way while living in a world that quite strongly agreed with this point of view. Jealousy is a natural and normal emotion for any of us to have, and I am not afraid to admit that it frequently popped up for me in the first few years of my poly journey. While I never got to the "slash-the-tires" place of jealousy, I definitely got those shots of adrenaline coupled with fear of loss shooting through my veins on a number of occasions. Meditation helped center me and balance out my emotions. More importantly, it got me in the right mindset to discuss jealousy constructively with my partners. Eureka! Awesome stuff!

Is this all sounding a little too woo-woo for you? Need more proof? The proof, as they say, is in the pudding! Research shows people do their best work when they're being their best selves — happy, fulfilled, and engaged. Let's look at the stats:

— Mindfulness practice enables people to better handle interpersonal stress and create positive outcomes in difficult situations (Daphne et al., 2012).

— Just 80 minutes of mindfulness practice reduces anxiety 24%, and improves executive functioning and working memory (Zeidan et al., 2010).

— Those who practiced mindfulness reported greater life satisfaction, resilience, wellbeing, and immune response than those who did not practice (Bajaj et al., 2016).

You have nothing to lose by giving compassion meditation a try! Heck, give ANY meditation a shot. You can also experiment with meditation websites like my favorite, Headspace.com. To get you started, I have techniques to set you off in the right direction right now. Let's do this! And remember...

> **KINDNESS TO OTHERS BEGINS WITH KINDNESS TO ONESELF. TRY TO AVOID JUDGING THE EXERCISE OR THINKING IN TERMS OF PROGRESS OR NOT — AND THE SAME GOES FOR INTERACTIONS IN EVERYDAY LIFE.**

COMPASSION MEDITATION TECHNIQUES

Time Required — 15 minutes daily

How To Do It
I recommend listening to the audio of this guided meditation that you can download from Dr. Emma Seppala's website (creator of this meditation; link can be found in the Resources). I have included a script of the meditation to help you follow it yourself or teach it to others.

Body Position
Close your eyes. Sit comfortably with your feet flat on the floor and your spine straight. Relax your whole body. Keep your eyes closed throughout the whole visualization and bring your awareness inward. Without straining or concentrating, just relax and gently follow the instructions.
   Take a deep breath in. And breathe out.

Receiving Compassion-Loving-Kindness
Keeping your eyes closed, think of one of your partners — a person close to you who loves you very much. Imagine that person standing on your right side, sending you their love. That person is sending you wishes for your safety, for your well-being, and happiness. Feel the warm wishes and love coming from that person towards you.

Now bring to mind the same person or another person — another partner perhaps or someone else — who cherishes you deeply. Imagine that person standing on your left side, sending you wishes for your wellness, for your health, and happiness. Feel the kindness and warmth coming to you from that person.

Now imagine that you are surrounded on all sides by all the people who love you and have loved you. Picture all of your friends and loved ones surrounding you. They are standing sending you wishes for your happiness, well-being, and health. Bask in the warm wishes and love coming from all sides. You are filled, and overflowing with warmth and love.

"The purpose of a relationship is to remember more of who we are... in 'relation' to another."

— BRUCE D. SCHNEIDER

Sending Compassion-Loving-Kindness to Loved Ones

Now bring your awareness back to the person standing on your right side. Begin to send the love that you feel back to that person. You and this person are similar. Just like you, this person wishes to be happy. Send all your love and warm wishes to that person.

Repeat the following phrase three times silently:

May you live with ease, may you be happy, may you be free from pain.

Now focus your awareness on the person standing on your left side. Begin to direct the love within you to that person. Send all your love and warmth to that person. That person and you are alike. Just like you, that person wishes to have a good life.

Repeat the following phrase three times silently:

Just as I wish to, may you be safe, may you be healthy, may you live with ease and happiness.

Now picture another person that you love, perhaps a relative or a friend. This person, like you, wishes to have a happy life. Send warm wishes to that person.
Repeat the following phrase three times silently:

May your life be filled with happiness, health, and well-being.

Sending Compassion-Loving-Kindness to Your Metamour
Now think of your partner's partner, someone you may or may not know very well and toward whom you may have mixed feelings at this time. You and this person are alike in your wish to have a good life.
Send all your wishes for well-being to that person, repeating the following phrase three times silently:

Just as I wish to, may you also live with ease and happiness.

Sending Compassion-Loving-Kindness to All Living Beings
Now expand your awareness and picture the whole globe in front of you as a little ball.
Send warm wishes to all living beings on the globe, who, like you, want to be happy:

Just as I wish to, may you live with ease, happiness, and good health.

Take a deep breath in. And breathe out. And another deep breath in and let it go. Notice the state of your mind and how you feel after this meditation.

When you're ready, you may open your eyes.

"Obstacles are those frightening things you see when you take your eye off the target."
— CURT CARLSON

Abridged Version Compassion Skill

Like many people, I occasionally have trouble sleeping — whether it's anxiety about a troubling poly-related event in my life, worry about a loved one, or simply an annoying song getting stuck in my head. For years, I have used this super-short yet effective compassion meditation to help me relax my mind, calm the other noise in my head, and eventually get back to sleep. Heck, I just used it last night! Here it is:

May I be happy.
May I be peaceful.
May I forgive myself.

That's it! Easy to remember. Easy to implement. Easy to do. And usually within 5–15 minutes, I'm back to sleepy-town. Feel free to create an abridged version of any of the compassion meditations that we explored here during a challenging or triggering moment. Perhaps have it at the ready for when you excuse yourself to the restroom so you can have five minutes to yourself, or at your desk right before a difficult phone call. You can use it virtually anywhere, and no one has to be the wiser that you are quietly calming your mind, finding inner peace for yourself, and rocking your emotional and mental well-being on the spot. You owe it to yourself — and your loved ones — to learn how to find your own path to happy, centered, and able to be as compassionate and loving as possible!

SUMMARY OF COMPASSION SKILL

When we practice compassion for ourselves, we open up our hearts as well as get our own physical heartbeat to slowly calm down. Practicing compassion for our partners who love us, and then our metamours who love them (and perhaps us too today or tomorrow), allows us to create magic! Remember that you have control over your own thoughts, feelings, and experiences.

Make that "target" your own happiness in the form of practicing compassion, love, and kindness — for yourself and your wider circle! You can welcome more personal happiness in your own life practicing this method, and then share that abundance with other people. Next, let's take a closer look at your core personal values that guide you!

CHAPTER 5

Strategy Three: Commitment To Your Core Personal Values

"It is better to follow the Voice inside and be at war with the whole world, than to follow the ways of the world and be at war with your deepest self."

— MICHAEL PASTORE

Who are you really? And what do you REALLY want? I suspect you want loving, healthy, awesome relationships, or you would not be reading this book. I'll venture a guess that you want healthy OPEN relationships as well, possibly polyamorous ones, which is why you're reading this SPECIFIC book.

COMMITMENT TO YOUR CORE PERSONAL VALUES

In this section I assume that open, healthy relationships are one of your core values. Great! Act on that value, even if you don't feel like it. No seriously! When you are having a wonky moment, it can really help to remember what your core values are. Ask yourself: How would a person who holds this as a core value act? Then do your best to behave in that way. Try to act as a thoughtful, open, inclusive, and caring poly partner would. Channel that energy. Because energy attracts like energy, you will also attract those that value those same qualities. It's a win-win!

"Each moment describes who you are and gives you the opportunity to decide if that's who you want to be."
— Bruce D. Schneider

Be the person you truly want to be in the world. Every day you get to reinvent yourself, and be a better version of yourself. Who do you want to show up as? In terms of the subject of this book, do you want to be a frazzled, crazed, drama-creating, stressed-out person who gets in a jealous rage and potentially damages your relationships? Or do you want to come from a compassionate, loving, understanding place, practicing patience with yourself and others, and create inner peace for yourself and a feeling of safety for others?

Figure that out. And then act accordingly. Some things are just that simple.

Do you value inner peace or order in your life? If you want to get your life in order, screw the goals and skip the plans. Jump straight to values — your non-negotiables for how you do business, treat your loved ones, and do life. Everything else falls under this. Sure, plans are good and goals are fine. But even megalomaniacs have goals and well-designed plans. That's not enough to live a good life. If you really want to kick ass in life, you have to have values — good ones — to make a positive dent in this universe.

Not sure what your core values are? Well, let me give you a roadmap to figure that out. This is a critically important step on our journey together. It will greatly assist you in not only your consensually non-monogamous lifestyle, but every single aspect of your life! With your goals as your guidepost, every decision you make will become easier. Have a tough choice? Which option aligns more perfectly with your current stated values? It may give you more fulfillment, inner peace, and joy to select the choice that most closely aligns with these core values.

COMMITMENT — CORE PERSONAL VALUES TECHNIQUES

> *"If you don't know where you're going, any road will take you there."*

Values are the principles that people live by, the things that make them tick and drive them. If you don't know where you stand on work, friends, or family when an opportunity to succeed at something comes along, you'll screw it up. Trust me. I've been there.

Think of a value like a compass that is guiding you on the journey of your life that provides much needed direction. Again, value-guided direction in our life is different from setting goals. Goals are the coveted milestones that you come up with AFTER you determine what your values are, and what direction you are headed. THEN you can determine goals that fall within that framework.

As we do this work, it is important for us to recognize that there are two kinds of values: Fear-Based and Conscious-Based.

Two types of values:

FEAR-BASED = HAVE To's — These values spur you to take action to avoid something. "I have to do this... or else."

CONSCIOUS-BASED = WANT To's — These values allow you to take positive action.

It's important to realize when you're choosing from passion or fear, consciously or not.

Keep this in mind as you do the following Values Assessment exercise.

How To Figure Out Core Values?

Find a quiet place, set aside at least a half an hour, get a pen and paper or a computer, and consider your responses to these questions:

General

— Imagine you get to watch your own funeral. What do you want your loved ones to say on the mic? What was your life about?
— Think about a time when your life was really good. What value was being expressed or honored?
— Think about a time when you were upset. What value was being challenged?
— When do you compromise your values? Why?
— Think about what you MUST experience in life. Why is that so important?
— Recollect a person or superhero whom you admire. What do you imagine this mentor/hero's stated values would be?

Open Relationships

— Deep down inside, what is important to you as a partner in open relationships?
— What do you want to stand for as a partner in open relationships?
— What sort of personal strengths and qualities do you want to cultivate as a partner in open relationships?
— How do you want to behave as a partner in open relationships?

Here's a list of values that you can use as a guide to select from for those values that are most important to you. Because this is not an exhaustive list, feel free to think of other values that you would place on your own list.

Accomplishment	Leadership
Absence of Pain	Loyalty
Abundance	Mental Health
Adventure	Nature
Altruism	Openness
Autonomy	Orderliness
Authenticity	Personal Growth
Avoidance of Conflict	Partnership
Beauty	Physical Appearance
Clarity	Power
Commitment	Privacy
Community	Professionalism
Connection	Recognition
Creativity	Respect
Emotional Health	Romance
Environment	Safety
Excellence	Security
Family	Self-Care
Flexibility	Self-Expression
Freedom	Self-Mastery
Friendship	Self-Protection
Fulfillment	Self-Realization
Fun	Sensuality
Health/Fitness	Service
Holistic Living	Spirituality
Honesty	Trust
Humor	Truth
Integrity	Well-being
Intimacy	Vitality
Joy	Other:

After looking at this list, narrow it down to the top five values that resonate with you. After you have your five, then cut down your list to your all-time top three core values. Make a note of these top three to five values in a place that you can find easily. Be prepared to refer to it often, especially as we do this work together and then later when you go out to meet jealousy head on.

What impact are you going to make in your relationships and the world around you? Here's hoping you make the impact that you want to make, aligning with your values as your guide when times get tough.

> *"Everyone has his own specific vocation or mission in life; everyone must carry out a concrete assignment that demands fulfillment. Therein he cannot be replaced, nor can his life be repeated, thus, everyone's task is unique as his specific opportunity to implement it."*
>
> —Viktor Frankl

SUMMARY OF COMMITMENT TO CORE VALUES SKILL

Your relationships will be easier to navigate if you focus on aligning your actions with your core values. First, you need to determine what your core values are. Once you assess your core values, you can then commit to acting in ways that support those values, as well as support your mission in your relationships and in your life. You might be surprised at how everything starts to flow more naturally for you once you determine your core values, and as you continue every day and in every way to align your behavior and actions with these values.

We cannot control the people around us, but we can change the way we relate to them. View every interaction as an opportunity to train, tame, and soften the mind.

CHAPTER 6

Strategy Four: Communication

"True success lies not in just being yourself, not in doing the best you can, but in knowing the two are the same."

— BRUCE D. SCHNEIDER

We need to decide whether or not to talk about our jealousy. We might decide that our jealousy was nothing to get so upset about, that our relationships are good, and that we don't need anything to change. Our jealousy has passed and nothing more needs to be done. Basically, don't sweat the small stuff.

The thing is, it's not always small stuff.

Sometimes jealous thoughts and feelings can be helpful. Jealousy may point to some real issues that we must deal with in our relationships. Effective communication about our jealousy can help improve our relationships! Here we delve deeper into this topic of communication.

COMMUNICATION *(if needed)*

It is a running joke in the world of open relationships that the mantra for success is "communication, communication, communication." I whole-heartedly agree that if you truly want to not only survive but thrive in some form of open relationship, it is imperative that you work pro-actively at continually improving your communication skills.

Unfortunately, using your old patterns, habits, and go-to's for communicating with your partner(s) may not get you to where you need to be. Ignoring your problems, your challenging feelings, or your partners certainly isn't going to be a very effective strategy either.

I would like to challenge the assumption that the feeling of jealousy is to be avoided at all costs. Trying to avoid a natural human feeling such as jealousy is like telling ourselves that we are WRONG to be a normal, functioning human being. We are making ourselves wrong for being human! How silly is that? Why do we do this to ourselves?

> *"Love yourself for who you are now.*
> *Believe in yourself for who you have the power to become."*
>
> — Karen Salmansohn

Additionally, it is erroneous to assume that just because we have always had a knee-jerk reaction to jealousy in our past, that we cannot learn new, more effective strategies for more productively and constructively working through this emotion. In fact, we CAN learn to deal effectively with our emotions, and these strategies can help!

I offer you your first tool:

COMMUNICATION TOOL #1

KNOW WHEN TO HOLD 'EM

***Red Light:* PUSH PAUSE BUTTON ON CONFLICT**
I have intentionally included the words "if needed" next to the word "communication" because it is quite possible that the earlier techniques we discussed (Mindset, Defusion, Compassion, and Commitment) may work so well, that you find that you don't really need to open

a dialogue with your partner at all! There is a hidden skill in knowing when NOT to broach a subject. As Kenny Rogers says in his song "Ya Gotta Know When To Hold 'Em" — in this case, it's know when to hold your words. Words matter! Jealousy conversations and concerns can become emotionally charged pretty quickly. In the heat of the moment, people sometimes say or do things that can damage their relationships. Proceed with caution when embarking on this type of conversational adventure. Make sure that you are centered, balanced, have thought through your intention of having the dialogue, and what your goals are before you broach the subject.

So here are two massively helpful tips for you to consider implementing in your mind before you even open your mouth to communicate:

Make Good Choices

I have a spoiler alert for you about this thing called "life":

YOU ARE RESPONSIBLE FOR YOU, YOUR HEALTH, AND YOUR HAPPINESS.

Boom! Consider saying that to yourself five times every morning until you have absorbed it into your soul, mind, and subconscious.

Let's discuss how you can take responsibility for yourself by making good choices.

1. **Regulate emotions.** Calm down before communicating, and make it easier for your partners to regulate their emotions. For example, wait until they are well-rested, calm, well-fed, and able to focus on the conversation. Cunning Minx of PolyWeekly refers to this as

being mindful of "B.N.C.," or do you or your partner need a Blowjob, Nap, or Cookie before you can have a constructive conversation? Be mindful of yours and your partner's BNCs.

Another reason to hit the pause button before talking: When jealousy is coursing through your system, that's when it is most likely to hijack your brain. It can take up to 20 minutes for you to get back to a centered place where you can speak calmly, rationally, and get the full use of your conscious brain back. Give yourself permission to take a moment to yourself to calm down and re-group. You will thank me later for reducing the amount of drama you allow in your own life by doing this simple step. When you see drama happening in your life, you can take a moment and ask yourself: Am I creating this drama myself? How am I contributing to this situation? When all you see is the green fog of jealousy, be patient with yourself and take a step back when emotions are frenzied and you notice you have lost the ability to think straight.

> *"All experiences are opportunities for growth."*
> — BRUCE D. SCHNEIDER

2. **Remember your relationship goals.** Think about what you want from your relationship, and what kind of response you want from your partner(s), and choose the type of communication accordingly. Sounds simple, right? In the abstract, thinking about that is no problem. In the heat of the moment, though, sometimes you have to stop and think:

What Are Your Relationship Goals? Do you want your partner to say, "I love you" and give you a hug? Then don't start an argument, silly!

When you see that written, it may seem like common sense. But when sparks are flying and emotions are highly charged, it can be incredibly difficult to remember. I urge you to take a deep breath, assess where you are, and consider the outcome that you desire. Then think through — do you want to be "right," or do you want to connect with your partner(s)? Do you want to "win" (essentially making the other person lose/making them "wrong"), or do you want to increase the love and happiness that you have in your life and with your partner(s) while creating a deeper understanding between you? These are important mind-shift moments that can create magic!

Don't forget what we learned earlier in this book: Are connection, open relationships, being impeccable with your word, or spreading love instead of hate components of your current-day value system? If so, then don't forget to ensure the intention behind your actions is aligning with those stated values. This is simple, yet hardly ever easy. I know that you are strong, smart, and can do anything that you set your mind to!

You got this! You can do it!

> *"Each of us is greater and wiser than we appear to be (to ourselves and others)."*
> — Bruce D. Schneider

Yellow Light: SLOW DOWN & THINK BEFORE YOU SPEAK

Before we get started on talking about HOW to speak to your partner, let's go over some typical default ways that humans tend to communicate, and create some ground rules for your communication. Nothing highly constructive ever gets done without a solid understanding of the game we are playing. A fantastic guide also helps light up our path to success so that we don't veer off course into old, destructive habits. First, we will consider…

4 Ways to Communicate

People often respond to conflict and relationship dissatisfaction in four ways: Exit, Neglect, Loyalty, and Voice (ENLV) that I'll outline below.

- **EXIT:** *"I'm leaving."* Exiting means formally separating, moving out of a joint residence, deciding to "just be friends," or breaking up.

- **NEGLECT:** *"I'm ignoring you and your needs."* Ignoring your partners or spending less time together, refusing to discuss problems, withdrawing affection, treating your partners badly either emotionally or physically, criticizing your partners for things unrelated to the real problem, "just letting things fall apart," or developing other relationships in preparation for exit are all parts of neglect.

- **LOYALTY:** *"I hope things get better."* Expressing loyalty often includes waiting and hoping that things will improve, "giving things some time," hoping for progress.

- **VOICE:** *"I would like to talk about this."* Using voice means discussing problems, compromising, seeking help from a therapist, suggesting solutions to problems, expressing oneself to create and ease understanding, asking your partners what is troubling them, or trying to make positive changes.

Let's face it: We have ALL used these above strategies at some time in our lives, or experienced them on the receiving end. Deciding to break up or formerly separate from a partner is a huge decision not to be taken lightly, because breakups can be highly traumatic. You should definitely not make this type of decision in the heat of the moment, but wait until after thoughtful consideration has been taken and a (hopefully) respectful dialogue with your former love has occurred. After all, you have been head over heels in love with this person before and care deeply about them, and perhaps still do! The ground rules we will discuss momentarily can still apply to that potential conversation as well. But I digress...

Unless you decide to exit/breakup/separate from your partner, from this point forward I am suggesting that you focus on the last communication style of giving voice to conflict when and if you decide to open up a dialogue with your partner. Why? Because this "voice" style of communication has the greatest chance of success for a positive and constructive outcome. Additionally, it puts you in the driver seat of your life instead of playing victim or giving power over to the other players by watching and waiting to see what they will do. Be courageous! Be you! Speak up and speak your mind when you need to, asking for what you need. I know first-hand how scary it can be to do that, but you will feel 10 times taller and wiser when you are on the other side of that conversation.

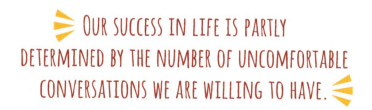

> Our success in life is partly determined by the number of uncomfortable conversations we are willing to have.

DOs & DON'Ts for
Actionable & Constructive Conversations

DO

Big tip and critical guideline here! Please pay attention! When we talk with our partners about our jealousy, it helps to have an actionable conversation. An actionable conversation focuses on things that we can do, changes that we can make, things that our partners can do, or changes that our partner can make. Here are some general DOs and DON'Ts for actionable conversations...

- Have an actionable conversation based on needs and values
- Disclosing (e.g., disclosing feelings, needs, and/or values)
- Deepening Understanding (eg., asking questions, discussing problems, trying to understand different perspectives)
- Problem Solving Activity (eg., suggesting solutions to problems, trying to make changes, trying to reach an understanding)
- Seeking Outside Help (eg., seeking help from a support group, coach, or counselor)

DON'T

- Engage in emotional distancing (e.g., give the "silent treatment", give cold looks, withdraw affection, refuse intimacy as punishment)
- Engage in verbal aggression (e.g., express excessive anger, make accusations, be sarcastic, be rude, yell, argue)
- Engage in manipulation (e.g., induce guilt, test the partner's loyalty, make ultimatums)
- Engage in violence (e.g., slam doors, break dishes, throw possessions out of the house, threaten to harm a partner, push, slap, hit)

- Engage in demand-withdrawal patterns (e.g., one partner makes a demand, the other partner withdraws creating a toxic and destructive cycle)
- Threaten to disrupt relationships (e.g., threaten to leave or break up with your partner, demand that your partner end a relationship with someone else, threaten to be violent towards someone your partner is spending time with)

I know what you may be thinking: The problem with lists of DOs and DON'Ts is that things don't always work out as planned. Right? It's easy to make a list of DOs and DON'Ts, but it can be much harder to put the DOs and DON'Ts into practice. So now we are ready to move onto some specific communication tools for success to help us do just that.

"In spite of warnings, nothing much happens until the status quo becomes more painful than change."
— L. J. Peter

Green Light: GIVING VOICE TO CONFLICT
All right, we're ready to give ourselves the green light to communicate with our partner. Perhaps you have already started. If our conversations about jealousy seem to fall into a rut or we seem to keep getting stuck on certain topics, it's possible to use special communication techniques to help us move forward. One special technique is called nonviolent communication. Another special communication technique is called active listening. Let's start with the former.

COMMUNICATION TOOL #2
NONVIOLENT COMMUNICATION

You've done your homework: You have prepped your mental state, completed a self-check to see if you need to work on yourself first, know the potential landmines that you could step on, and have learned how to avoid them. Awesome! Even so, you still fear your relationship might be deteriorating based on where you currently are, and how you (and possibly your partner) are feeling and thinking. Not awesome. So that means it's time to TALK it out. Then hopefully hug-it-out afterward — yeah baby! Keep the goal of hugging-it-out afterward in mind as we proceed. OK? Let's do this!

Nonviolent communication (NVC) is one of the most powerful tools available for transforming our lives and world. These principles have been incredibly helpful to me in dealing with challenging relationship situations in my life. NVC was developed by Dr. Marshall B. Rosenberg, who has introduced it to individuals and organizations world-wide.

Nonviolent Communication (NVC) Primer
(reprinted with permission — source listed under "Resources")

Nonviolent Communication (NVC) has been described as a language of compassion, and as a tool for positive social change. NVC gives us the tools to understand what triggers us, to take responsibility for our reactions, and to deepen our connection with ourselves and others, thereby transforming our habitual responses to life. Ultimately, NVC involves a radical change in how we think about life and meaning.

Nonviolent Communication is based on a fundamental principle: Underlying all human actions are needs that people are seeking to

meet. Understanding and acknowledging these needs can create a shared basis for connection, cooperation, and more harmonious relationships on both a personal and global level. When we are able to understand each other at the level of our needs we can cultivate compassion because, on the deepest levels, the similarities between us outweigh the differences.

When we focus on needs — without interpreting or conveying criticism, blame, or demands — our deeper creativity flourishes, and solutions arise that were previously blocked from our awareness. At this depth, conflicts and misunderstandings can be resolved with greater ease.

The language of Nonviolent Communication includes two parts: honestly expressing ourselves to others, and listening empathetically to others. Both are expressed through four components — observations, feelings, needs, and requests. Practicing NVC involves distinguishing these components from judgments, interpretations, and demands, and learning to embody the consciousness embedded in these components. This compassionate approach allows us to express ourselves and hear ourselves and others in ways more likely to foster understanding and connection. It allows us to support everyone involved in getting their needs met, and to nurture in all of us a joy in giving and in receiving.

NVC also includes empathic connection with ourselves — self-empathy. The purpose of self-empathy is to support us in maintaining connection with our own needs, thus encouraging us to choose our actions and responses based on self-connection and self-acceptance.

The Components of Nonviolent Communication

Observations

Observations are what we see or hear that we identify as the stimulus to our reactions. **Our aim is to describe what we are reacting to con-**

cretely, specifically, and neutrally, much as a video camera might capture the moment. This helps create a shared reality with the other person. The observation gives the context for our expression of feelings and needs.

The key to making an observation is to separate our own judgments, evaluations or interpretations from our description of what happened. For example, if we say: "That time when you were rude to me," the other person may be confused or disagree. Alternately, if we say: "When you walked in, you did not say hello to me," the other person is more likely to recognize the moment that is described.

When we are able to describe what we see or hear in observation language without mixing in evaluation, we raise the likelihood that the person listening to us will hear this first step without immediately wanting to respond, and will be more willing to hear our feelings and needs.

Learning to translate judgments and interpretations into observation language moves us away from right/wrong thinking. **Emphasizing observation helps us take responsibility for our reactions by directing our attention to our needs as the source of our feelings, rather than to the faults of the other person.** In this way, observations emerge as a crucial building block towards more meaningful connection by paving the way towards greater connection with ourselves and with others.

Feelings

Feelings represent our emotional experience and physical sensations associated with our needs that have been met or that remain unmet. Our aim is to identify, name, and connect with those feelings. The key to identifying and expressing feelings is to focus on words that describe our inner experience rather than words that describe our interpretations of people's actions. For example: "I feel lonely" describes an inner experience, while "I feel like you don't love me" describes an interpretation of how the other person may be feeling. When we express our feelings, we continue the process of taking responsibility for our experiences, which helps others hear what's important to us with less likelihood of interpreting it as criticism or blame of themselves. This increases the likelihood that they will respond in a way that meets both our needs.

A list of feelings you may want to reference and explore is available earlier in this book in chapter two on page 33.

Needs

Our needs are an expression of our deepest shared humanity. All human beings share key needs for survival like hydration, nourishment, rest, shelter, and connection. We share many other needs, though we may experience them to varying degrees, and may experience them more or less intensely at different times.

In the context of Nonviolent Communication, needs refer to what is most alive in us: our core values and deepest human longings. Understanding, naming, and connecting with our needs helps us to both improve our relationship with ourselves and foster understanding with others, so we are all more likely to take actions that meet everyone's needs.

The key to identifying, expressing, and connecting with needs is to focus on words that describe shared human experience, rather than words that describe the particular strategies to meet those needs. **Whenever we include a person, a location, an action, a time, or an object in our expression of what we want, we are describing a strategy rather than a need.**

For example: "I want you to come to my birthday party" may be a strategy to meet a need for love and connection. In this case, we have a person, an action, and an implied time, and location in the original statement. The internal shift from focusing on a specific strategy to connecting with underlying needs often provides people with a sense of power and liberation. We are encouraged to free ourselves from being attached to one specific strategy by identifying the underlying needs and exploring alternative strategies.

For most people, feelings arise when our needs are met or not met — something that happens at every moment of life. **Our feelings are related to the trigger, but they are not caused by the trigger: their source is our own met or unmet needs. By connecting our feelings with our needs, we can take full responsibility for our feelings, freeing us and others from fault and blame.**

By expressing our unique experience in the moment of a shared human reality of needs, we create an opportunity for another person to see our humanity and experience empathy and understanding for us.

A list of needs you may wish to explore is listed on the next page. I provide the list as a resource for identifying and experiencing your own needs and guessing others' needs. The needs on this list appear in their most abstract, general, and universal form. Introspection will allow individuals to find the specific nuance and flavor of these broader categories to more fully describe their own unique experiences.

Requests

Making requests allows us to assess how likely we are to get cooperation for particular strategies we have in mind for meeting our needs. Our aim is to identify and express a specific action that we believe will serve this purpose, and then check with others involved about their willingness to participate in meeting our needs in this way.

In any given moment, it is our connection with another that determines the quality of their response to our request. When using NVC, our requests are connection requests, intended to foster connection and understanding, and to determine whether we have sufficiently connected to move on to a solution request that seeks a specific outcome.

For example, a connection request might be: "Would you tell me

List Of Needs

Connection
acceptance
affection
appreciation
belonging
closeness
communication
community
companionship
compassion
consideration
consistency
cooperation
empathy
inclusion
intimacy
love
mutuality
nurturing
respect/
  self-respect
safety
security
stability
support
to know and
  be known
to see and be seen
to understand and
  be understood
trust
warmth

Physical Well-being
air
food
movement/
  exercise
rest/sleep
safety
sexual expression
shelter
touch
water

Honesty
authenticity
integrity
presence

Play
humor
joy

Peace
beauty
communion
ease
equality
harmony
inspiration
order

Autonomy
choice
freedom
independence
space
spontaneity

Meaning
awareness
celebration of life
challenge
clarity
competence
consciousness
contribution
creativity
discovery
efficacy
effectiveness
growth
hope
learning
mourning
participation
purpose
self-expression
stimulation
to matter
understanding

how you feel about this?" An example of a solution request is: "Would you be willing to take your shoes off when you come in the house?" The spirit of requests relies on our willingness to hear a "no" and to continue to work with ourselves or others to find ways to meet everyone's needs.

Whether we are making a request or a demand is often evident by our response when our request is denied. A denied demand will lead to punitive consequences; a denied request most often will lead to further dialogue. We recognize that "no" is an expression of some need that is preventing the other person from saying "yes".

When we trust that we can find strategies through dialogue to meet both of our needs, "no" is simply information to alert us that saying yes to our request may be too costly in terms of the other person's needs. We can then continue to seek connection and understanding to allow additional strategies to arise that will work to meet more needs.

Two things increase the likelihood that our requests will be understood: using language that is as concrete and action-oriented as possible, and that is truly a request rather than a demand. For example, "I would like you to always come on time" is unlikely to be doable, while "Would you be willing to spend 15 minutes with me talking about what may help you arrive at 9 am to our meetings?" is concrete and realistic.

While a person may assent to the former expression ("Yes, I'll always come on time"), our deeper needs — for connection, confidence, trust, responsibility, respect, or others — are likely to remain unmet. If someone agrees to our request out of fear, guilt, shame, obligation, or the desire for reward, this compromises the quality of connection and trust between us.

When we are able to express a clear request, we increase the likelihood that the person listening to us will feel that they are given a realistic choice in their response. While we may not gain immediate assent to our wishes, we are more likely to get our needs met over time because we are building trust that everyone's needs matter. Goodwill flourishes within an atmosphere of such trust, and with it a willingness to support each other in getting our needs met.

Learning the skills to make clear requests and shifting our consciousness to making requests in place of demands can be very challenging for most people. Many find the request part to be the hardest, because of what I think of as a **crisis of imagination** — a difficulty in identifying a strategy that could actually meet our needs without being at the expense of the needs of others.

Even before considering the needs of others, the very act of coming up with what we call a positive, action-oriented request is challenging. We are habituated to thinking in terms of what we want people to stop doing (e.g., "Don't yell at me"), and how we want them to be (e.g., "Treat me with respect"), rather than what we want them to do (e.g., "Would you be willing to lower your voice or talk later?")

With time, and a deeper connection to our needs, our creativity expands to imagine and embrace more diverse strategies. This fourth step in NVC — making a concrete request — is critical to our ability to create the life we want. In particular, **shifting from demands to requests requires a leap in both focus and faith: we shift from focusing on getting our needs met, to focusing on the quality of connection that will allow both of our needs to truly matter, and ultimately also to be met.**

Empathy

Expressing our own observations, feelings, needs, and requests to others is one part of Nonviolent Communication. The second part is empathy: the process of connecting with another by guessing their feelings and needs.

Empathic connection can sometimes happen silently, but in times of conflict, verbally communicating to another person that we understand their feelings and that their needs matter to us can be a powerful turning point in challenging situations.

Demonstrating that we have such understanding does not require us to sacrifice our own needs. Connecting empathetically with another person can be a catalyst for meeting our needs for understanding, connection, contribution, and more. At the same time, empathy can be a powerful tool to help us meet the other person's needs. The ability to understand and express the other person's feelings can aid us in finding strategies that meet both of our needs.

The language of NVC often helps us relate with others, but the heart of empathy is in our ability to compassionately connect with our own and others' humanity. Offering our empathic presence, in this sense, is a means through which we can meet our own needs. It is a gift to another person and to ourselves of our full presence.

When we use NVC to connect empathetically, we use the same four components in the form of a question, because we can never be certain of what is going on inside of other people. **We respect that the other person is the ultimate authority on what is going on for them.**

Our empathy may meet other people's needs for understanding, or it may spark their own self-discovery. We may ask something like:

Observation: *When you [see, hear, etc.]...*
Feeling: *Are you feeling...*
Need: *Because you need...*
Request: *And would you like...?*

In an ongoing process of dialogue, there is often no need to mention either the observation (it is usually clear in the context of communication) or the request (because we are already acting on an assumed request for empathy). We might get to guessing a request only after we have connected more and are ready to explore strategies.

In the process of sharing empathy between two people, when both parties connect at the level of feelings and needs, one or both parties often shift their attention in a way that transforms the situation. This can lead to a shift of needs or generate new reserves of kindness and generosity. In seemingly impossible situations, these shifts can even open us to remarkable bursts of creative solutions that were unimaginable when clouded by disconnection.

Self-Empathy

Both expression of our own feelings and needs, and empathetic guesses of others' feelings and needs are grounded in an inner awareness which is at the heart of nonviolent communication. Practicing self-empathy is the best way we know of to nurture inner awareness.

In self-empathy, we bring the same compassionate attention to ourselves that we give to others when listening to them using NVC. This means listening through any interpretations and judgments of ourselves that we are making so that we can clarify how we are feeling and what we need.

This inner awareness and clarity supports us in expressing ourselves to others, or receiving them with empathy. It allows us to make a request to ourselves about where we want to focus our attention.

The practice of NVC entails an intention to connect compassionately both with ourselves and with others, and an ability to keep our attention in the present moment — which includes being aware that sometimes in this present moment we are recalling the past, or imagining a future possibility.

Often self-empathy comes easily, as we access our sensations, emotions, and needs to attune to our current status. However, in moments of conflict or reactivity to others, we may find ourselves reluctant to access an intention to connect compassionately, and we may falter in our capacity to attend to the present moment.

Self-empathy at times like this has the power to transform our disconnected state of being and return us to our compassionate intention and present-oriented attention. With practice, many people find that self-empathy alone sometimes resolves inner conflicts and conflicts with others as it transforms our experience of life.

Summary of Principles of Nonviolent Communication
(From http://www.wikihow.com/Practice-Nonviolent-Communication)

- State concrete actions you observe in yourself or the other person.
- State the feeling that the observation is triggering in you. Or, guess what the other person is feeling, and ask.
- State the need that is the cause of that feeling. Or, guess the need that caused the feeling in the other person, and ask.
- Make a concrete request for action to meet the need just identified.

NVC Basic Pattern:

When I observe A,
I feel B
because I need C.
Would you be willing to D?

    1. When I observe... (examples)

see	notice
hear	remember
feel	think about

2. I feel... (examples)

annoyed	embarrassed
angry	tired
disgusted	sad
uneasy	vulnerable
detached	scared
stressed	hurt

3. Because I need... (examples)

safety	to be valued
respect	support
empathy	trust
honesty	play
love	acceptance
mutuality	autonomy

4. Would you be willing to... (doable, related to the present, not a demand, e.g., "...spend more time with me this weekend," or "reassure me about your feelings")

I cannot say enough good things about using nonviolent communication in your relationships to ease handling virtually ANY potentially charged conversation. Speaking from experience, NVC has helped me transform a terrifying and damaging situation into a beautiful and healthy exchange. Use it earnestly after studying the concepts here, and you will see what a powerful tool it can be for you as well. We are now ready for our final communication tool: Active Listening.

COMMUNICATION TOOL #3
ACTIVE LISTENING

It's almost ironic that the most important aspect of communication is not speaking, but listening. Listening is at the heart of great, compassionate communication. We attract people into our lives for a reason, for a season, or a lifetime, but always for a growing and learning experience. The more we listen, the more we learn.

Here's an exercise for you: Try out practicing the 80/20 rule of you doing 20% of the listening, and let your partner(s) do 80% of the talking. Try remembering the acronym W.A.I.T — which stands for Why Am I Talking? Our partners are gifts in our life. Try listening intently to them and the unique gifts that they are sharing with you.

There are three levels of listening with our end goal being the last described below: Active and Intuitive Listening.

Subjective Listening — Listening is based on the agenda or needs of the listener. Whatever is said is related back to the listener. This is what most of us do 99% of the time! e.g., "Oh and that reminds me of the time I...."

Objective Listening — The listener is completely focused on the person who is speaking. Objective listeners are not thinking about how the conversation relates to them personally because they are focused on what the other person is saying. While this level of listening is very effective, it doesn't truly get to the heart of the matter. Paraphrasing back what someone is saying falls under this category. It's one-dimensional. It does help the speaker feel heard, which is awesome!

Active/Intuitive Listening — The listener is listening to all sensory components and intuitively connecting to the speaker's real message. Active/Intuitive listeners pay attention not only to what the speaker is saying, but also to the speaker's tone of voice, energy level, feelings, etc. These listeners also notice what's NOT being said. This is the most powerful form of listening, in part because it allows the listener to really connect with the speaker. This type of listening also helps validate the other person for the thoughts and feelings that they share. Because Active/Intuitive listening can help to create an empathetic connection, it can feel very empowering and energizing to the speaker, and often the listener as well.

Active Listening Basic Pattern:
- **Listen** in order to fully understand what your partner is saying to you.
- **Ask Questions** that help you get more information. For example, "What did you mean when you said...?"
- **Reflect** what you heard your partner say so you can be sure you heard correctly.
- **Offer Empathy** for what your partner is saying.

Action + Purpose of Action

Listening — Be there for your partner by focusing on what your partner is saying.

Asking — Check how well you understand what your partner is saying.

Reflecting — Show that you understand what your partner is saying.

Empathizing — Help your partner feel cared for and understood.

Effective listening is more than just skill. It's also a matter of attitude. To be an effective listener, you must accept your partners for who and what they are, not what you want them to be.

I AM ALWAYS LISTENING, LEARNING, AND GROWING.

SUMMARY OF COMMUNICATIONS SKILL

Wow are you setup for success now! You have learned — in a very short amount of time — some of the most powerfully effective communication tools available! As you can see, even though these techniques are quite simple, they are not always easy in the moment. They all take practice, practice, practice (to go with communicate, communicate, communicate).

Now I ask you to reflect for a moment: How important would it be for you to have amazing, compassionate, loving, and connected conversations with your partner instead of drag-out, tearful, yelling matches where no one wins and feelings are hurt? And how powerful would it be to have those kinds of dialogues even in the face of the crazy, stressful emotion of jealousy? You can do this — if you put in the time, effort, commitment, and work. Have faith in yourself, and have faith in your partner.

FAITH IT UNTIL YOU MAKE IT.

SECTION III
NOW WHAT?

CHAPTER 7

Putting It All Together

"The best way to teach love is to be love."
— BRUCE D. SCHNEIDER

Congratulations! Wow! It is quite an accomplishment to get to this point on our journey together! I am elated and so proud that you have stuck with it and charged on through the exercises and learnings contained herein this humble book. Investing in yourself and your education, personal growth, and relationships says a lot about you. It shows that you value and love yourself enough to optimize both your own life, and your interactions with your loved ones. You are helping make a beautiful vision — what was once only a dream — become your reality. This is your life! You have the power to make it great. *You go!*

I TRULY BELIEVE THAT WE CAN IMPROVE THE QUALITY OF OUR LIVES BY IMPROVING THE QUALITY OF OUR RELATIONSHIPS.

I believe that at the end of each of our life journeys, it is love and the quality of our connections that we will cherish and hold dear to our hearts, no matter which path we choose to get there (monogamous, polyamorous, or otherwise). Being vulnerable and truly connecting means knowing who you are and having the courage to share your authentic self with others. Expressing our authentic selves includes admitting that sometimes we have challenging and confusing emotions.

So many of us fear and even dread the human and very normal emotion of jealousy. Even though I have pointed it out over and over, it bears repeating because it is a crucial concept: Jealousy is just a feeling — it will not kill you. Your mind may be telling you that you can't withstand this challenge of jealousy, but I am here to tell you this:

YOU CAN STAND IT.

And as we have shown throughout this book, you can use jealousy as a tool for positive change — not only positive change within your relationships, but positive change within yourself. You have a choice every day in how you choose to show up in the world, and how you choose to react to the events and people around you, including your chosen family, your polycule.

> "The greatest freedom is the freedom of choice."
> — Bruce D. Schneider

I know I've thrown a lot of information and a lot of work at you in the previous chapters, and some of it may stir up some strong emotions. This work may activate some unfinished business from your past or family of origin. You might feel sadness at the loss of a sense of safety in a relationship, or guilt at how you have handled your frenzied, volatile emotions in the past. That was yesterday, done and past, and right now we are living in the present.

> *"Yesterday is history, tomorrow is a mystery, but today is a gift. That's why we call it the present."*
>
> — A. A. Milne

Changing your behavior is neither a linear process, nor is it instantaneous. As you make the skills you've learned here an integral part of your life, you'll find that you won't get it right every time. At points, you will falter, other times fear will overtake you. You'll try and sometimes you'll inevitably fail — everyone does. That's totally normal! The important thing is not that you be perfect every time, but that you continue to learn from both your triumphs and your mistakes. Each positive step in the right direction towards effective change helps make you the warrior that you are, the champion that you are becoming. Keep going!

Remember that what you're doing is like climbing a mountain, except that no one ever gets to the top. No one is so articulate, zen, and anxiety-free that they can always come up with exactly the right words and actions to deflect getting triggered by a jealousy attack. Be gentle and forgiving with yourself. As you work your way up this mountain of change, you'll probably glance up and think "Oh gosh, I've still got so far to go!" That is when you need to take a moment to turn around and look back towards the place you started. You've come a long way, baby!

> *"You have dealt with so much and done the best that you can. Take a moment to appreciate how strong you are."*
>
> — Karen Salmansohn

Ideas from the
Loving Without Boundaries (LWB) Community

I have been blessed to be surrounded by an incredible community of wise, consensually non-monogamous veterans in the trenches who support my work. You all seriously rock! I decided to take the following question to the LWB community.

What are some of your biggest challenges when it comes to dealing with feelings of jealousy? Also what has worked for you in the past to overcome them?

Here are their answers:

"When it comes to dealing with strong emotions like jealousy, I try and remind myself that feelings are not facts. I feel it helps me to see things more objectively." — REBECCA

"I always go back to the actions of the person/people I'm with. If I go back to their actions, and they spend time with me and act in a considerate manner, then I work on myself. If I feel jealous because someone isn't spending enough time with me or isn't acting in a considerate manner, then I re-evaluate what's going on." — WENDY

"Jealousy is usually a sign of that I am feeling insecure about the way my partner feels about me because of either time apart, or because he is seeing someone new. Something that has helped me regulate these emotions is I keep a blog... one of my posts is a running list of texts, snippets from emails, or words that my partner has sent to or said to me that make me feel special, loved, and cherished. When I am feeling jealous or neglected, I go read this blog post and the ongoing list of love words. This usually helps bring my brain and heart back in alignment and reassures me of the reality of the love that my partner has for me." — ANGEL

Thank you, LWB community, for sharing your beautiful, inspiring, and awesome ideas! I am incredibly grateful to be surrounded by such fantastic, brave, and courageous people who are all looking out for each other and sharing their wisdom and insights. Love you guys!

With that, I will add my personal tip that I use in my own life.

Kitty's Special Polyamorous Jealousy-Busting Bonus Tip

Picturing my love(s) in the arms of another or whispering sweet nothings to them can fill me with those jealous pangs. But I will tell you this: I have done A LOT of work on myself in becoming a sex-positive person growing up in a sex-negative world — and still recovering from Catholic school to boot! It is crucial for me to remember that I do not OWN my partners but that we CHOOSE to share our lives together. Also, I want them to feel safe being honest with me and telling me about other partners and adventures.

So I remind myself that I love sex. That's right, I just said it. I love sex!

And if my partner(s) are having sex with others, that means that they are becoming better and more sensitive lovers, even learning new sexy tricks or bonus maneuvers. The freedom to explore with a variety of lovers adds to my partners' happiness of also being sex-positive and getting to expand their sensuality. In essence, it is a win-win-win because they bring home all of the learning, goodness, positive sexual energy, and happiness back home to me! Love breeds more love! And I love fantastic sexual adventures and mind-blowing sex. More of that please! Yes, and thank you!

You can consider trying on that thought process for size in your consensually non-monogamous life. It has helped me greatly and always serves to calm me down and helps create more magic in my life.

> "Believe in what you want so much
> that it has no choice but to materialize."
>
> — Karen Salmansohn

Now, how are you going to create more magic in your life? I can assure you that with every step you take to learn and use skills that will disarm the potential destructive outcomes of experiencing jealousy, you will be restoring the very core of your being — your integrity and sense of self-worth. That precious inner peace you may have mourned was never really lost — just misplaced for a while in the throes of a jealousy attack.

It has been waiting for you. Go re-claim it. Use your new tools, attitudes, and behaviors to take control of your emotional well-being and rock your relationships!

ADDITIONAL HELP ON YOUR JOURNEY

One-On-One Coaching

Would you prefer to have someone hold your hand through this process? I would be delighted to help you along your amazing journey and guide you to success and a more love-filled, stress-free life. I have a thriving and fulfilling coaching practice as a Certified Professional Coach (CPC), specializing in relationship coaching for people who want to find or are trying to maintain unconventional and alternative relationships. I work with wonderful people just like you every day, and it is an honor to serve you.

Please reach out to me at kitty@lovingwithoutboundaries.com to inquire about having an initial Discovery Session with me where we learn where you are on your journey, uncover any blocks to your success, and discuss strategies to get you where you want to ideally be.

Also feel free to connect with me just to say hi and tell me your thoughts about this book. I'd absolutely LOVE to hear from you! You are part of my rocking and amazing community now that you have read the words and insights that I have shared with you here. Thank you for being here.

Group Coaching via Workshops and Online Courses

In the winter of 2017, I will begin turning the teachings of this book into an online course scheduled to be released in late spring of 2018. Prior to that, I will be doing my part to offer this teaching as a live workshop at polyamory conferences around the country and eventually the globe, as well as at events in the Washington, DC area. Come to a workshop, take part, have fun, and say hi! I love meeting curious, spectacular, brave people just like you! You're awesome! And lastly thanks for reading this book. I am grateful for your time and effort, and hope that these new tools prove useful for you. I wish you peace, love, and happiness.

> *"Life is speedily short. Don't waste a nanosecond on thoughts and things that don't make you happy."*
>
> — KAREN SALMANSOHN

RESOURCES

BOOKS

8 Things I Wish I'd Known About Polyamory (Before I Tried It and Frakked It Up)
By Cunning Minx of PolyWeekly.com

Emotional Blackmail
By Susan Forward, Ph.D., and Donna Frazier

Get Out Of Your Mind and Into Your Life: The New Acceptance and Commitment Therapy
By Steven C. Hayes

The Happiness Track: How to Apply the Science of Happiness to Accelerate Your Success
By Emma Seppala (Science Director of Stanford University's Center for Compassion and Altruism Research and Education and creator of the Compassion Meditation in Chapter Four)

The Happiness Trap: How to Stop Struggling and Start Living: A Guide to ACT
By Russ Harris

I Need Your Love, Is That True?
By Byron Katie

Nonviolent Communication
By Marshall Rosenberg

Rising Strong
By Brené Brown

Stories from the Polycule: Real Life in Polyamorous Families
By Dr. Elisabeth Sheff

WEBSITES

The Entrepreneur Fitness Academy (Mindset) created by Mike Goncalves
MikeGoncalves.com

How To Be Happy, Dammit. created by Karen Salmansohn
Notsalmon.com

Kelly Cookson Teachings
kellycookson.info

Nonviolent Communication Summary (NVC): A Concise Guide to NVC
by Inbal and Miki Kashtan
http://www.wanttoknow.info/inspiration/nonviolent_communication_summary_nvc

Polyamory Weekly
polyweekly.com

A Poly Heart Blog by Angel Barbie
Apolyheart.blogspot.com

Scott Dinsmore TedX Talk
https://www.youtube.com/watch?v=jpe-LKn-4gM

WikiHow — Practice Nonviolent Communication
http://www.wikihow.com/Practice-Nonviolent-Communication

BIBLIOGRAPHY

Bajaj, B., and N. Pande "Mediating role of resilience in the impact of mindfulness on life satisfaction and affect as indices of subjective well-being." *Personality and Individual Differences* (2016): 93, 63-67.

Brown, Brené. *Rising Strong*. New York: Spiegel & Grau, 2015.

Cookson, Kelly. Kelly Cookson website: Retrieved 1 Feb. 2016 <kellycookson.info>.

Davis, Daphne, and Jeffrey Hayes. "What are the benefits of mindfulness?" *American Psychological Association website* (2012): <http://www.apa.org/monitor/2012/07-08/ce-corner.aspx>.

Forward, Susan, and Donna Frazier. *Emotional Blackmail*. New York: HarperCollins Publishing, 1997.

Grohol, J. "How Common is Cheating & Infidelity Really?" *Psych Central* (2013): Retrieved 6 Oct. 2017 <https://psychcentral.com/blog/archives/2013/03/22/how-common-is-cheating-infidelity-really/>.

Martins, A., M. Pereira, R. Andrade, F. M. Dattilio, I. Narciso, and M. C. Canavarro. "Infidelity in dating relationships: Gender-specific correlates of face-to-face and online extradyadic involvement." *Archives of Sexual Behavior* (2016): 45(1), 193-205.

Rosenberg, Marshall. *Nonviolent Communication*. 3rd ed. Encinitas, CA: Puddledancer Press, 2015.

Seppala, Emma. Meditation website: Retrieved 20 Jan. 2017 <emmaseppala.com/gift-loving-kindness-meditation/>.

Van Dyne, L., S. Ang, K. Y. Ng, T. Rockstuhl, M. L. Tan, and C. Koh. "Sub dimensions of the four factor model of cultural intelligence: Expanding the conceptualization and measurement of cultural intelligence." *Social and Personality Psychology Compass* (2012): 6(4), 295-313.

Zeidan, F., S. K. Johnson, N. S. Gordon, and P. Goolkasian. "Effects of brief and sham mindfulness meditation on mood and cardiovascular variables." *The Journal of Alternative and Complementary Medicine* (2010): 16(8), 867-873.

ABOUT THE AUTHOR

Kitty Chambliss is a polyamorous and sex-positive speaker, author, educator, relationship coach, activist, and founder of **Loving Without Boundaries (LWB)**. Since 2012 LWB has over 220 blog posts and 70 podcasts to date. Kitty's work has been featured in *Stories From the Polycule, Multiamory, SwingTowns, PostModern Woman,* the *YoushareProject,* the upcoming book *It's Called "Polyamory": Coming Out About Your Nonmonogamous Relationships,* and other publications around the globe. She has also been a special guest panelist and speaker on radio shows, international and national conferences, and more. She is a dual-certified (CPC and ELI-MP) relationship coach having graduated from **The Institute for Professional Excellence in Coaching (IPEC)**. Kitty is thrilled to be bringing her book: *Jealousy Survival Guide* out to the world. **Kitty has made it her life's mission to make thriving relationships — even unconventional ones — attainable to everyone.**

Within two years of authoring her blog, Kitty's work received the **Bad Girl Bloggers Award** and now has 4,000+ followers. Within the first three weeks of production, her LWB podcast reached the status of **New & Noteworthy** on iTunes under the categories of Sexuality and Health. She enjoys interviewing world-renowned authors, speakers, educators, therapists, and authorities in the fields of ethical non-monogamy, relationships, and even a "coming out coach."

Kitty has worked with many clients privately over the past three years helping everyone (from singles to triads and beyond) have more deeply fulfilling love lives.

When she's not coaching clients, writing a blog post, or capturing a podcast interview, Kitty loves to pretend she's awesome at pole fitness dancing and being a rock star musician. She also loves immersing herself in new cultures, and savoring inspiring conversations over a great glass of wine with loved ones.

NOTE: Kitty writes under a pseudonym partly due to discrimination in the world. Kitty is working to help create more tolerance and awareness of stigmatized lifestyles such as alternative relationships. Also, due to the nature of her sex-positive work, Kitty occasionally gets unwelcome advances and harassment. These make the one step removed nature of a pseudonym desirable and necessary at this time.

If you would like to invite Kitty Chambliss to speak at an event for your organization, please make contact via lovingwithoutboundaries.com.

GET INVOLVED & GET GUIDANCE

If you enjoyed this book or found it useful, I'd be incredibly grateful if you'd post a short review on Amazon. Your support really does make a difference. I read all of the reviews personally so I can get your feedback and make this book even better.

At **Loving Without Boundaries**, we are committed to being a valuable resource to the community offering free tools, resources, articles, and interviews from various voices on the topic of consensual non-monogamy, healthy relationships, and rocking your unconventional love life.

Feel free to join our amazing community by going to:

LovingWithoutBoundaries.com

There you can follow us at:
The Blog
The Podcast
iTunes
Facebook
Instagram
Pinterest
Twitter @polytalkbykitty

Also get on the waiting list for online courses being offered in the future!

Want More Specialized Help?

We also offer one-on-one relationship and transformational coaching services. Go to the link to learn more and schedule a 30-minute consultation.

Made in the USA
Middletown, DE
06 April 2018